EMPATH

Discover 50
Emotional, Physical and Spiritual Energy

Alison L. Alverson

Also by Alison L. Alverson

Chakra Series Book 1
Chakra Healing For Beginners: The Complete Guide to Awaken and Balance Chakras for Self-Healing and Positive Energy

Chakra Series Book 2
Chakra Healing For Beginners: Discover 35 Self-Healing Techniques to Awaken and Balance Chakras for Health and Positive Energy

Empath Series Book 1
Empath: An Extensive Guide for Developing Your Gift of Intuition to Thrive in Life

Empath Series Book 2
Empath Workbook: Discover 50 Successful Tips To Boost your Emotional, Physical And Spiritual Energy

Standalone

Emotional Intelligence : 21 Effective Tips To Boost Your EQ (A Practical Guide To Mastering Emotions, Improving Social Skills & Fulfilling Relationships For A Happy And Successful Life)

Watch for more at www.alisonalverson.com.

Table of Contents

Empath Workbook: Discover 50 Successful Tips To Boost your Emotional, Physical And Spiritual Energy (Empath Series Book 2) 1
Introduction 2
The Empath's Secret Weapons For Controlling Energy 15
Tips For Not Losing The Me In We—Relationships And The Empath..29
The Underestimated Challenges Empaths Face And How To Overcome Them..42
The Mystical Way: The Empath And Spirituality...........................48
Essential Tools and Techniques Every Empath Should Know......63
The Last Tip Empaths Should Never Forget 68
A Bonus Chapter Of My Book: | CHAKRA HEALING FOR BEGINNERS..71
Energizing Your Chakras Through Guided Meditation 73

© **Copyright 2020 by Alison L. Alverson - All rights reserved.**

This document is geared towards providing exact and reliable information in regards to the topic and issue covered. The publication is sold with the idea that the publisher is not required to render an accounting, officially permitted, or otherwise, qualified services. If advice is necessary, legal or professional, a practiced individual in the profession should be ordered.

- From a Declaration of Principles which was accepted and approved equally by a Committee of the American Bar Association and a Committee of Publishers and Associations.

In no way is it legal to reproduce, duplicate, or transmit any part of this document in either electronic means or in printed format. Recording of this publication is strictly prohibited and any storage of this document is not allowed unless with written permission from the publisher. All rights reserved.

The information provided herein is stated to be truthful and consistent, in that any liability, in terms of inattention or otherwise, by any usage or abuse of any policies, processes, or directions contained within is the solitary and utter responsibility of the recipient reader. Under no circumstances will any legal responsibility or blame be held against the publisher for any reparation, damages, or monetary loss due to the information herein, either directly or indirectly.

Respective authors own all copyrights not held by the publisher.

The information herein is offered for informational purposes solely and is universal as so. The presentation of the information is without a contract or any type of guarantee assurance.

The trademarks that are used are without any consent, and the publication of the trademark is without permission or backing by the trademark owner. All trademarks and brands within this book are for clarifying purposes only and are owned by the owners themselves, not affiliated with this document

Introduction

Do you remember a time when you felt so alive with all the wondrous energy of the universe? You could tap into the energy that ran through everything and you were intensely curious about all that was around you. You were tuned-in to your surroundings and you could feel your empathic and creative gifts awakening. You likely even had vibrant dreams and visions that came true. Your outer life felt magical and your inner life was nothing short of whimsical and enchanting. You were enamored with nature and, like a sponge, you soaked up all the information you could about subjects like science, animals, and art. You might even have expressed yourself through dance and music. It was a wonderful time when everything seemed possible.

But then, something happened as you began to share what you knew with those around you. People in your life were skeptical and maybe even frightened or angry. As they questioned your gifts, you began to hide them away. You even denied they existed, as you felt an increasing pressure to be "normal". Maybe you feel that this denial of who you really are is devastating and you can't keep doing it. You find that you're drained of energy by engaging with toxic people who continue to hurt you so deeply. You find yourself asking why the world has to be so harsh and you're wondering if your gifts are even real. You can't seem to find anyone who understands you and you might even wonder if this is all there is to life—misunderstanding and pain.

But perhaps now you feel your inner voice screaming out in desperation, "That's enough!" You finally realize that you just can't pretend anymore. Now, you sense you're experiencing an awakening and you're looking for answers and deeper meaning. As you look around, you start noticing what seem to be signs and synchronicities that are guiding you to a new path, a path where you can be yourself, where you don't have to change yourself to fit in. Still, you're not quite sure of the next step. You want a life where you can thrive in the warm glow of your unique gifts. You need to heal yourself and discover how to be healthy, happy and connected.

In my first book, *Empath*: An Extensive Guide for Developing Your Gift of Intuition to Thrive in Life, I shared how you can recognize if you have this gift—and it is a gift—and how you can tap into it. I know exactly what you're going through because I've experienced this myself. That's why I decided to create this practical workbook to help empaths on this critical journey of self-discovery and, more importantly, self-acceptance.

With this workbook, you'll have a useful guide that will assist you with the difficulties and sensitivities that are so common for empathic people. It will be a great reference guide that will help you learn and grow as an empath and the helpful quizzes, journal prompts, and reflection exercises will give you practical advice on how to connect to your heart space, as you embark upon the all-important journey of self-discovery. You've already taken the first step—you're looking for help. You want to bring the magic back. Now it's time to take the next step—start using this book to grow into the healthy and happy empath you were always meant to be!

Taking this journey alone is not recommended so I highly encourage you to join our friendly community on Facebook to maximize the value you receive from this book. What often helps a lot is connecting with other like-minded empaths. People you can relate to, get support from and learn from on how to navigate this world with your unique gift. This can be an excellent support network for you.

It would be great to connect with you there,

Alison L. Alverson

To join, visit: www.facebook.com/groups/empathsupportcommunity/[1]

---

[1] http://www.facebook.com/groups/empathsupportcommunity/

Seven Powerful Crystals Every Empath Should Have

Are you feeling overwhelmed with other people's emotions?

Would you like to protect and heal your energy?

Being an empath means absorbing both the positive and negative energies

This can be both a blessing and a curse

The good news is that crystals with their unique characteristics and vibration can actually help

To balance your emotions, protect your energy and keep you grounded with these 7 powerful crystals, visit: https://bit.ly/2Y8cIkp

Keys to Understanding Your Empathic Ability

There is some vital information about empaths and energy that I want to talk about before we get into controlling the energy around you. I have found this very helpful for a better understanding of how to control the energy I sense around me. Let's begin by taking a short self-assessment quiz about the way you respond to the energies you sense around you. Mark the following statements true or false:

1. I frequently get overwhelmed or anxious. True? False?
2. Arguments or yelling make me physically ill. True? False?
3. I am drained by crowds and need alone time to revive myself. True? False?
4. I am overstimulated by noise, odors, or non-stop talkers. True? False?
5. I overeat to cope with stress. True? False?
6. I tend to socially isolate myself. True? False?
7. I need to replenish myself in nature. True? False?
8. I need a long time to recuperate after being with difficult people or energy vampires. True? False?
9. I feel better in small cities or the country than in large cities. True? False?
10. I prefer one-to-one interactions or small groups, rather than large gatherings. True? False?

If you answered true to 5 or more of these statements, then you're likely an empath, but even more, if you marked certain statements as true—1, 2, 4, 5, and 8 among them—you might be having difficulty managing the energy you sense so strongly. So, let's talk a little about energy.

What is energy?

Every living thing exudes energy. It is expressed by a subtle electromagnetic field that surrounds the organism. For an empath, this energy field is larger than most and its boundaries are not as well-defined as they are for other people. Therefore, it is important to understand how energy functions for the empath before we delve into how energy manifests.

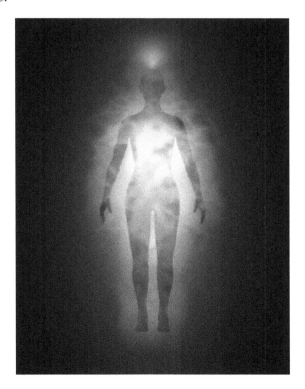

Energy is basically a form of fuel our bodies need to perform any activity. As you engage in activities, you spend the energy your body has stored and, therefore, you need to be re-energized at certain points. Now, many people can be re-energized by the mere act of engaging with other people, but most empaths tend toward introversion and, therefore, they feel drained as they engage with the people around them. Additionally, the energy field of an empath tends to overlap with literally everyone and everything around them. That makes energy management that much more important for the empath. They frequently need to get away from crowds and spend time alone, often in nature, in order to re-energize. That makes it very important for empaths to set healthy boundaries and to understand and respect their needs.

Journal Prompt: Take a moment at this juncture to write in your journal. If you don't have one, now is a good time to start one. Write down five things or situations that make you feel drained of energy. Next, write down five ways in which you are able to recharge your batteries. Do you notice anything about what drains you? Do you notice any patterns about how you are best able to recharge your batteries? Write down your thoughts.

How Sensitive are You?

Now that we've defined energy, let's talk a little more about how the empath manages that energy. Because the energetic field of an empath overlaps with other people and their surroundings, it can become very difficult to define your own energy versus that of other people. Additionally, because this energy carries with it information about emotions, thoughts, and intentions, it's very easy to be overwhelmed, confused, or even disturbed by this stimulation coming at you from all sides. To put it more simply, an empath is like a sponge, soaking up the energetic information all around them. Because empaths don't have the same kinds of filters and boundaries others have, they often absorb those energies they encounter in their surroundings.

Now, there is a spectrum of sensitivity. Not all empaths feel the energetic sensations around them at the same level. In order to manage the energetic fields you're able to sense, it can help to understand where you fall on the spectrum of sensitivity. To do that, check which of the following apply to you:

1. Do people describe you as naturally shy? — Yes? No?
2. Are you easily influenced by others? — Yes? No?
3. Do you find it difficult to say no? — Yes? No?
4. Do people often approach you to ask for your help without provocation? — Yes? No?
5. Do you often feel ignored or overlooked? — Yes? No?
6. Do you often feel your sense of self or your purpose is confused? — Yes? No?
7. Do you feel the emotions of others as if they are your own? — Yes? No?
8. Are you a people pleaser? — Yes? No?
9. Do you dislike being touched? — Yes? No?
10. Do you sometimes find it difficult to identify your own feelings and desires? — Yes? No?
11. Do you avoid crowds? — Yes? No?
12. Do you often feel phantom aches or pains? — Yes? No?
13. Do you need to be alone to recharge? — Yes? No?
14. Do you feel overwhelmed in places, like hospitals, where there is an emotionally charged atmosphere? — Yes? No?
15. Do you feel drained after being social? — Yes? No?
16. Are you hypersensitive to the actions and/or opinions of — Yes No

others? Yes No

17. Do you have problems setting a boundary with others? Yes No

18. Are you usually the giver and rarely the taker? Yes No

19. Do you frequently experience mood swings? Yes No

20. Do you accidentally or easily take on the moods and traits of other people when you are around them? Yes No

21. Do you avoid loud places or people? Yes No

22. Are you overly sensitive to violent or emotional media? Yes No

23. Do you keep your own problems to yourself? Yes No

24. Do you have a large capacity for understanding other people? Yes No

25. Do you feel driven to heal other people or help them solve their problems? Yes No

26. Are you highly intuitive? Yes No

27. Are you introverted? Yes No

28. Do you prefer to stay home as much as possible? Yes No

29. Do you find it easy to tell if someone is being dishonest? Yes No

30. Does it seem like you attract people who take advantage of you? Yes No

31. Do you feel like you have difficulty fitting in? Yes No

		Yes?	No?
32.	Do you frequently feel lonely?		
33.	Do you prefer solitary activities?	Yes?	No?
34.	Do you dislike small talk or inauthentic interactions with others?	Yes?	No?
35.	Do you place an extreme value on your privacy?	Yes?	No?

The more questions you answered in the affirmative, the higher on the sensitivity scale you are as an empath.

Journal Prompt: Write down in your journal how many questions you answered in the affirmative, as well as your thoughts about how sensitive you are based on this scale:

- **1 - 12**: Low sensitivity
- **12 - 24**: Medium sensitivity
- **Above 24**: High sensitivity

Which Kind of Empath are You?

Regardless of where you fall on the sensitivity scale, it can help to know what kind of empath you are so you will have a deeper understanding of the kinds of energy you're receiving, as well as the sources of that energy. Knowing this can help you with energy management. There are six types of empaths and I have included a short description of each. If you would like more information to determine your type, please check my first book, *Empath: An Extensive Guide for Developing Your Gift of Intuition to Thrive in Life*

1. **Emotional Empath**: This is one of the most common types and, if you are easily able to detect the emotions of those around you and, more importantly, if you feel these emotions as if they are your own, this is your type.

2. **Physical/Emotional Empath**: This type of empath picks up on the energy of other people's bodies. They might feel, for example, a type of awareness in their own body in the area where the other person is having problems.
3. **Geomantic Empath**: This type of empath is finely tuned to the physical landscape. Often, these empaths feel inexplicably happy or uncomfortable in certain environments. It is because they are feeling a connection to the place. It may have to do with the history of the place—perhaps something tragic or joyful occurred there—or it might have to do with the sacred power of a place.
4. **Plant Empath**: This person intuitively senses what plants need. They have green thumbs and a gift for placing the right plant in the right place. They often choose to work in parks, gardens, or wild landscapes where their gifts go to good use.
5. **Animal Empath**: These empaths have a strong connection with animals and often devote their lives to caring for our animal friends. They have a gift for knowing what an animal needs and may also be able to telepathically communicate with animals.
6. **Intuitive Empath**: This person is easily able to pick up information about people by being around them. They can know immediately if someone is lying to them and they can provide all kinds of insight into the people around them.

Journal Prompt: Write in your journal the type of empath you feel you are and how that type of empathic ability presents challenges to your energy management. For example, if you are an animal empath, perhaps you feel intensely the pain of any kind of animal mistreatment. If you're a plant empath, you might feel the pain of deforestation on a physical level. Also, make a few notes about how you might be able to manage these challenges. Don't worry if you don't have any specific solutions right now, this book will help with that, but the goal is to get you thinking about your own situation and your own energy management strategy.

The Empath's Secret Weapons For Controlling Energy

Now that you have a good idea of your empathic type and level of sensitivity, let's look at how energy manifests itself for the empath.

Manifesting and Emotions

Because empaths have the ability to pick up on the emotions of other people or things in their environment, they can often feel bombarded by emotional energies. I know I did before I learned how to better manage incoming energy. With practice, you too can learn how to heal, project, work with, and amplify emotional energy, even negative emotional energy. Regardless of the type of empath you are, it is common for empaths to absorb the emotional energy to which they are exposed. This act, in and of itself, can make the people around you feel better. For example, people suffering from depression often feel better around an empath because they siphon off their negative energy. Well, that's great for the depressed person, but not so hot for the empath. This can create a situation where you are at the mercy of your own gift. But, with training, you can learn to take the emotional energy you're pulling from your surroundings and transform it, so it can be used to heal or manifest, as well as to project a happier emotional climate. Let's start with gaining control of your gift.

Tip #1—The Molten Empathy Technique: This technique can help you to free yourself of negative emotions and allow you to become accustomed to working with emotional energy. Use this technique whenever you feel an inexplicable negative emotion.

- **Breathe and go deep**: The first thing to do when you sense a negative emotion from your surroundings is to take a deep breath and look inside yourself to explore how that negativity is affecting your body. Negative emotions feel heavy, cloying, and/or dark, and it is that heaviness that is a clue. Locate where you feel it in your body and how it is holding you back.

- **Send the energy on its way**: The negative energy giving you that heavy feeling wants to go to the center of the earth, so take hold of it and send it on its way. At the center of the earth, it will be broken down to its purest form by the molten core. To send it on its way, visualize yourself pushing or draining or siphoning the energy down into the earth. See it flowing into the ground, past the roots and dirt, through the layers of fossils and rock, and into the liquid hot magma at the core of the earth. As you do, you will notice you feel lighter.

- **Pull in joy**: As you push out the negative emotional energy to the core of the earth, fill yourself up with the joy of blue skies, birds singing, and the celebration of life around you.

Practice this technique often, as it will help you to gain control over the way negative emotions affect you. In time, you'll be able to drain away negative energy before it is able to even touch you.

Journal Prompt: The next time you feel impacted by an inexplicable negative emotion, practice this technique and describe your experience. As you write about it in your journal, answer the following questions:

- What kind of environment were you in when you felt the inexplicable negative emotion?

- What did you experience/feel?

- Could you identify an origin for the feeling?

- How did you feel as you drained the negative emotion into the center of the earth?

- How did you respond to filling yourself with joy?

- What did you feel after the incident was over?

Continue to write your experiences with this in your journal each new time you are affected by inexplicable negative emotions. Notice the patterns that emerge. What are the common environments in which you tend to experience these feelings? Are there people around and, if so, how many and what are they doing? Are there animals or plants around? Do these feelings tend to emerge in environments where there is a tragic or intense history? Identifying these patterns will help you understand your own experiences with greater clarity.

Tip #2—The Projective Empathy Technique: This technique is something you can use to help other people feel better when they're experiencing negative emotions. With this technique, you can remove the charge of the negative energy and help the person calm down. It can work to help a desperate person feel hope, a sad person feel joy, or an upset person feel peace. Since you're connected to them through your empathic ability, you can use this to reverse the direction of the emotional energy and project your own positive feelings into their heart. To do this, you need a reserve of positive emotions. These positive emotions are stored in your memory, so all you have to do is remember a time when you felt joyful or peaceful or calm. But, you need to have these memories at the ready and it can help to write them down.

Journal Prompt: Write down a time when you felt the following positive emotions:

- Joy
- Peace
- Calmness
- Happiness
- Hope

To project these positive emotions, you need to do more than simply remember them. You need to let yourself feel these feelings again. So, as you look at your list of memories, go back and relive those moments when you felt the flow of strong, positive emotions surging through your being. Practice feeling these emotions often. Not only will they help you be ready when you encounter someone who needs your help, they'll help you feel better too!

When you do encounter someone—or something—who needs your help, take the following steps:

1. Breathe deeply and choose the emotion you want to project;
2. In your mind, recall the memory that will evoke that emotion—relive the memory as if it were happening right now;
3. Fill your heart with the emotion from that memory, let it flood your being and feel your body bursting at the seams with this positive emotion;
4. When you sense the emotional energy beginning to overflow the boundaries of your body, send it to the person who needs your help—visualize it shooting straight into their heart. Feel the connection between your heart and theirs. This will cause their negative energy to transform into the positive energy you've projected into their heart.

Journal Prompt: Yep, you guessed it. It's time to write your experience in your journal. I know you might be skeptical of journaling, but it has helped me so much. The benefit of it is that it will help you to keep track of the progress you will make towards gaining more control over the energy you're picking up on from other people or things. You'll begin to see that you're better able to notice when you're receiving negative energy and you'll get better and faster at defusing that negativity.

Tip #3—Manifesting with empathy: You can use your empathy to help manifest your heart's desire into reality. There are numerous techniques that have been described to help you manifest the things you most desire. These include using visualization and petitioning the universe, but what is really at work here is the emotional energy behind the desire. Emotion is like a universal language and feelings contain a lot of energy. That's why they are crucial for manifesting. As an empath, you're intimately connected to the heart of the universe, so when you feel something, you feel it so strongly you can almost feel it into existence.

Whatever technique you want to use to describe your desire—whether it's visualization or another technique, the key to making it manifest will be to let yourself feel the emotions around what you want. What will it feel like if you have achieved the thing or situation you want to manifest? Let the feeling flood your body. Feel the joy or triumph as you've done it, you've manifested what you want! Project that feeling into the universe and you will attract what you need to manifest your dreams.

Journal Prompt: Write down something you want to manifest. Describe it as fully as you can. If it is a thing, what is made of, what color is it, what does it do, how will you use it? If it is a situation, what is needed, how will it help you, what will it look like in its final form? Describe what it is you want to manifest in as much detail as you can. Now, it's time for a little meditation.

Tip #4—Visualization Meditation and Energy: Visualization meditation can create a powerful energetic field. It's as if you transform your life in your mind and it allows you to fully sense the emotional energy inherent in doing so. Here's what you do:

- Sit in a comfortable position. You don't have to sit in the lotus position, but you also don't want to fall asleep, so sit up, but be comfortable.

- Close your eyes and begin by focusing on your breath. Feel it entering through your nose, going down into your chest as you expand both your belly and your chest. Feel it rising back up through your bronchial tubes and exiting through your mouth. Do this for five breaths.

- Now, visualize what you want to manifest. See yourself with the thing you desire or in the situation you desire. Imagine you have just achieved it. How are you feeling—triumphant, joyful, happy, excited? Let those feelings flood your body. Feel them in your heart. See yourself smiling and feel that excitement you had when you were a kid and just got exactly what you wanted for your birthday. Feel those emotions running through your entire body. Let yourself smile or giggle at the joy in your being. Visualize how having this will change your life.

- Express gratitude for this visualization practice and the happiness you have felt. Thank the universe for all it provides, for all you have right now, and allow the feelings of gratitude to infuse through your entire body. Feel those feelings of gratitude as they burst out of your body and enfold, first, those you love, then your community, then your city, state, country, and planet. Finally, send those feelings of gratitude out to the whole universe.

- Now, focus once again on your breath. Breathe deeply again for five breaths, and when you're ready, open your eyes.

The energy produced by this kind of visualization technique is a powerful tool for anyone, but that power is magnified when it is utilized by an empath.

Emotions and Health

I've been talking about how emotional energy can affect the empath, but let's take a deeper dive into how emotions and health are connected. This is something very important for the empath to understand because they are so strongly affected by emotional energy. To have good emotional health, it is necessary to first be aware of your thoughts, feelings, and behaviors, and how all of these are connected. It's also important to learn how to cope with stress because, let's face it, there will be difficult times in life. People who are able to cope with stress in a healthy way feel good about themselves and cultivate healthy relationships. But, even if you're someone who does have good emotional health, there are many changes in life that can disrupt that and lead to strong feelings of sadness or stress.

Even good changes that you want in your life can also cause stress. For example, you might be excited to move into a new house, but there's a lot of work that comes with moving and, on top of your already busy schedule, this can cause additional stress. Your body responds to this stress, regardless of whether it's good or bad. This is the mind/body connection that can lead to health problems if you don't understand how to manage your emotional energy.

Poor emotional health can result in numerous other health problems. The thing to understand about how your brain works is that it isn't able to distinguish between good or bad stress, it just sees stress and it activates the appropriate systems in the body to respond to that stress. What happens when you're stressed is that your brain activates what is called the sympathetic nervous system. This is the system that prepares you to either fight or flee—it's referred to as the fight or flight response. When this is activated, a series of changes occur in the body. Your heart rate increases as does your blood pressure, your eyes dilate, blood is shunted to the body's core, and a variety of corticosteroid hormones (adrenaline and cortisol, to name two) are released to give you the strength you need to either fight hard or run fast. Once the danger has passed, the parasympathetic nervous system is activated and it calms you down. When humans were living in the wild, where they could be eaten by a lion at any moment, these systems were necessary for survival. Sure, there are still times when your life might be in danger, but for the most part, in our modern world, these systems cause more problems than they solve.

The constant activation of your sympathetic nervous system can result in a number of health problems. It weakens your body's immune system, making you more likely to suffer from colds and other infections. You also are not as likely to take good care of yourself when feeling stressed. You might not exercise, you're less likely to eat well and you might abuse substances, like alcohol, tobacco, or other kinds of drugs. Stress can also manifest itself in a variety of symptoms, including back pain, chest pain, constipation or diarrhea, dry mouth, fatigue, headaches, high blood pressure, insomnia, heart palpitations (racing heart), sex problems, shortness of breath, stiff neck, lightheadedness, and an upset stomach, among others (familydoctor.org editorial staff, 2019). I discussed about this in details in my book, *EMOTIONAL INTELLIGENCE: 21 Effective Tips To Boost Your EQ (A Practical Guide To Mastering Emotions, Improving Social Skills & Fulfilling Relationships For A Happy And Successful Life)* .

Tips on How to Control Your Emotions

There are several ways to improve and maintain good emotional health. Let's look at a few of the best ways you can manage your emotions.

Tip #5—Awareness: The first thing you need to do to take control of your emotions is to be aware of them. You might think you are already aware of them, but you might just be aware of the initial emotion, which is often anger. To get to what's really bothering you, try this the next time you're triggered—stop and ask yourself why you're responding that way. For example, if you suddenly feel angry, stop and ask yourself what is the underlying emotion. Often, it's that you feel hurt. So, ask yourself what is the core emotion that's underlying your first reaction. To figure this out, turn around and look at the "little you" that's feeling this emotion. Visualize yourself there in the corner or sitting in the chair and ask yourself, "Why are you angry?" What comes to your mind? What does that little you say? Is he or she really afraid rather than angry and, if so, why? Listen to that little you because he or she reflects your core self. This is what you have come to believe about yourself through time. It's the product of what happened to you during your formative years. During that time, it's common to bury certain feelings deep inside and to construct core beliefs from those early experiences. To process these emotions, you have to get at these core beliefs.

Tip #6—Process your feelings: When your "little you" tells you why he or she is angry or fearful or ashamed or sad, listen and give yourself the comfort that you might not have received when you were young. Be as sympathetic and kind to yourself as you would be to your best friend. This was hard for me at first, but it has helped me so much and it will help you too. You'll find you're able to heal a lot of early trauma using this method. This is a vital technique for the empath because it will help you genuinely distinguish whether this is really your own emotion versus an emotion coming from someone else. Even if it is an emotion from someone or something else, you still need to process it through your system. Try the molten empathy technique to send those negative emotions to the earth's core and replace them with positive emotions. For your own emotions, try writing about them in a journal (see the prompt below), or perhaps, talking about them with a friend will help.

Do what feel comfortable for you, but remember as you process these emotions, you deserve to feel happy and at peace, so whatever core beliefs you might have adopted about yourself, they simply reflect a time when you didn't have the coping strategies you do now. Now, you can respond in a more positive way and you can truly heal.

Journal Prompt: To work on processing your own emotions, write about them in your journal. What core beliefs do they reflect? Are these beliefs true? If they are true, how can you let them go—how will you be different? If they are not true, what is true about you? Be sure to describe the context for the adoption of that core belief. How old were you? What did you feel? How did people around you respond? Can you give yourself the empathy you would give your best friend? Can you send love and positive emotions into your own heart? And can you love even that little shadow self of yours, the part of you that you don't want to acknowledge? Can you bring your shadow self into the light of love? For example, if you despise selfishness, it's because a shadow part of you is very selfish. You might have felt and really been, selfish at one point in time—who isn't—and, after being shamed for it, shoved that little selfish part of yourself into a deep corner of your mind. Bring him or her out into the light and love that selfish you. He or she was only trying to look out for you, to make sure you got what you need. Appreciate him or her and welcome them into the whole of you. This is how you heal.

Tip #7—Set appropriate boundaries: As an empath, it is vital that you learn to set appropriate boundaries with the people in your life. Because of your gift, people will undoubtedly be drawn to you to process their own emotions. They will use you as a sounding board to process their divorce or layoff or other kind of loss. And, you likely want to help them, but you have to do so in a way that is healthy for you. This means boundaries. When they come to process their emotions with you, set a time limit and stick to it. It's not that you don't love them or want to help them, but you have to take care of your own emotional energy. You cannot be all things to all people and this is particularly true if you expose yourself to things that will negatively affect your health. So, let them know in a kind way that you can only spend so much time with them. And schedule in some time for yourself after their visit, so you can process the emotions you experienced through them.

You should also set boundaries for yourself regarding how much time you spend on social media and news sites. There's a lot of happiness as well as despair in the world and you often hear more about the sadness than the happiness on the news. This is also true with social media. It's very easy for the empath to get caught up in other people's stories because you feel emotions so strongly. This is why it's better to limit the time you spend taking in these stories. Finally, for any boundary you set, be sure to stick to it. It's easy to say, "Well, it's just this once—he's really sad", but remember if you compromise your own health, you won't be able to help anyone.

Journal Prompt: Write down five activities you engage in that can cause you to feel overwhelmed. Now, set a boundary for each of these activities. Be specific—for example, if you engage in social media, set a one hour boundary for reviewing social media sites once a day and specify the time for that activity, like from 9 AM to 10 AM. Institute these boundaries in the next week.

Tip #8—Learn to Let it Go: While it's great to really feel the happiness of joyful moments, it's also really hard to actually experience the sadness of tragic moments. As an empath you get both, and so you have to learn to separate yourself from the emotions of those around you. You can do this by practicing separation. You did not lose a loved one, break up with your partner, or get a bad diagnosis. You are not the one actually having the difficult emotions that those around you are experiencing. To separate yourself and let go, you can use a ritual, like the molten empathy ritual discussed earlier, or you can find a confidant for yourself—someone you can process your emotions with who can help you let go. Feel the emotions passing through you but *let them pass through*. Don't grab hold of them, they aren't yours. Try visualizing the emotions passing through you as you're experiencing them. See them moving through and exiting your body. Once they've passed, express gratitude for the richness of the experience.

Tip #9—Cymatics and binaural beats: Another useful tool for the empath is the use of cymatics and binaural beats to produce altered states of consciousness. Research (Raghu, 2018) has shown that visualized sound can affect your emotional state. Cymatics is defined as the study of wave phenomena, especially sound, and their visual representations. One area of this research is binaural beats. Binaural beats are auditory illusions that are created by two different pure-tone waves with frequencies lower than 1,500 Hz. There should also be less than a 40 Hz between the two beats and these two tones are presented to the listener dichotically—one in each ear (headphones are required). These beats have been researched for over 170 years and they can produce different effects on human consciousness. Every brain is different and so there is no exact answer to what you will experience, but some of the common physical effects are:

- Total relaxation of the entire body;
- Vivid visualizations, colors, and patterns;
- Separation of the conscious and subconscious mind;
- Relief from stress, anxiety, and tension;
- Feelings of sedation, or not feeling the body at all.

For the empath, the use of cymatics and binaural beats is something that can help them to rid their body of negative emotions and/or help them to promote positive emotions. Often, the beats are paired with carrier frequencies selected from nature and holograms for an optimal experience that creates a deeply meditative state of relaxation.

The tips I've discussed in this chapter are key to helping the empath manage the emotional energy they come into contact with on a daily basis. These techniques will help you to process the intense emotions coming from other people, animals, plants, and/or the physical environment. These techniques will also allow you to manage the emotions which genuinely belong to you and even to heal some of the early trauma you may have experienced. Think of them as your secret weapon toolkit and use them often.

Tips For Not Losing The Me In We—Relationships And The Empath

Because empaths are extremely sensitive to the emotional energies around them, maintaining healthy relationships can be a minefield. Perhaps the first step for the empath is to make sure you have enough control over the emotional energies to which you are exposed, so you are not constantly reacting to what you're perceiving. Practicing the techniques in the previous chapter will help you to do this, but it's also helpful to fully understand energy bonds and how they affect you as an empath.

Understanding Energy Bonds

An energy connection is simply a link or bond between two people, but particularly for empaths, once that link is established, it is not easy to break. Empaths feel these connections very intensely. The empathic mother may feel the pain of her child in every area of her body. She may know when her child is hurt, even if that child is grown and living far away. There are even high-level empaths who felt the pain of a loved one being attacked in exactly the same area of the body they are being hurt, literally blow for blow. These energetic connections between the empath and their loved ones are mostly passive energetic connections formed by strong emotional bonds, but it's also possible to establish an energetic link through the ritual sharing of power like a reiki attunement or some other ritual mixing of energies. These ritual bonds can allow the empath to know if the other person is okay or hurt or if they need help, but they won't always know what's going on specifically. They may know the other person is lying, for example, but not about what. This can be a problem for the empath in their relationships. They may know the person is upset, but not why they are upset. The energy can be just as strong if the person is upset about getting a traffic ticket, as if they are having doubts about their romantic relationship.

Sharing an empathic bond can be beautiful, but it can also make the other person feel uncomfortable. "You see too much" and "know too much" are common complaints from partners of empaths. Those with whom the empath share a ritual bond often find that they can make an energetic connection simply by thinking about the empath. Some empaths report feeling different energetic signatures from different bonds. For example, one empath reports that the energy from some of their bonds feels as though someone is cupping their face in his hands or hugging them. They report a sensation of heat—without burning—in their skin in the areas affected. It's not an uncomfortable feeling, but it's definitely noticeable. Other bonded people might appear in the empath's dreams as a means of connecting energetically. It is also possible to have a non-bonded connection as an empath. These are connections where the person might reveal themselves to you in a way that is not energetic in nature. Perhaps you see them as a translucent shadow, for example, but you don't feel anything in your body.

The energetic connections you make as an empath are called cords and you are creating cords with each interaction. It's also possible for energetic hooks to form through your interactions. Hooks occur when someone is trying to 'hook' into your energy. They might do this by, for example, saying hurtful things in order to hook into you and take away your power. They can put you down, make you feel unloved, or even try to shame you. Once hooked into your energy, they can feed off of it in a sort of energetic vampirism and this can even negatively affect your health. That's why it's important to remember that hooks can only be implanted if you allow them. You might, for example, be seeking validation from this type of person, or you might think you can save them, but if you respond to them for those motives, you are giving them permission to set the hook, and once set, they can keep coming back for more. How do you know if someone has their hook in you? Here's a few examples of how you might feel:

- You have a needy friend who contacts you daily to tell you about their issues. After speaking with them, you feel drained or 'headachy.'

- You have a coworker who finds fault with everything and, when you're around them, you feel frustrated and stressed.

- Your partner belittles you and blames you for everything, but even though you know the relationship is unhealthy, you feel powerless to move on.

Journal Prompt: Think about the people with whom you have strong energetic bonds. List them and identify examples of when you have felt your connection with them. What is your energetic connection with them like? Do you know when someone you love is in trouble? Do you feel it in your body? Do you see them as a non-bonded shadow figure? How does the energetic connection manifest itself? Once you have identified how the energetic connection manifests itself, write a few words about each person and how you feel after having an interaction with them. Do you feel energized, loved, worried, headachy, powerless? We'll come back to this list later, but let's talk a bit about how you can protect yourself from the negative effects of energetic bonds.

Tip #10—Protecting Yourself from Unhealthy Energetic Bonds: There are a few simple exercises you can perform to sever the energetic cords attached to you. These rituals do not cut cords of love and they don't remove the person from your life, they just cut unhealthy energy connections. I use these techniques frequently.

Exercise #1: Severing connections

- Sit in a comfortable, but alert position.

- Focus on your breathing and follow your breath through five inhalation/exhalation cycles.

- Envision a white light that emanates from your heart center and surrounds your entire body. Feel its protective glow.

- Envision the energy cords connecting you to the other people in your life attached to your solar plexus. See yourself using a sword to sever the cords of energy; watch as the severed cords pull away from you. Send them back to the person they belong to and now turn to the severed attachments at your solar plexus.

- Envision the white light closing and healing the wound of the severed energy cords.

- Express gratitude for the healing powers of your own energy, as well as the gift that allows you to make such intense connections.

- Focus on your breath once again for five cycles.

- When you're ready, open your eyes.

Exercise #2: Removing Hooks

- Sit in a comfortable, but alert position.

- Focus on your breath and follow it for five inhalation/exhalation cycles.

- Envision yourself bathed in white light emanating from your heart space and encircling your entire body.

- Now, visualize the energy hooks and notice how deeply embedded they are in your tissues. Gently remove them one by one. Each time you remove a hook, send it back to the person it came from.

- Repeat the following statement when releasing each hook, "I release this hook and return it to the person who sent it to me. I hereby revoke any permission I may have given, knowingly or unknowingly, that allowed this person to take my power or drain my energy". Now visualize the hook returning to its owner.

- Look again to the area of where the hook was embedded and visualize the white light bathing the area and healing the wound.

- When all hooks have been removed and the areas healed, focus once again on your breath for five cycles.

- When you're ready, open your eyes.

You can repeat these energy reclaiming exercises as many times as needed. You might need to do either exercise for cutting cords or removing hooks more than one time if the other person is someone you have known for a long time. And if you are still in contact with the person, the cords can grow back, so you'll have to cut them often, but don't be fearful of this process. It's simply part of the process you need to do to protect yourself. Another step you can take to protect yourself is to erect a shield.

Exercise #3: Erecting a Shield

Once you've cut cords and removed hooks, it's good to follow up by erecting an energy shield around yourself. You should do this shielding visualization at least once each day. Simply sit in a comfortable position and envision yourself surrounded by a shield that protects you from incoming energy. Your shield might be a white light or a mirror. A mirror works well since it reflects the energy back to the source, but you can envision your shield in any form you like. You can envision yourself safe from unhealthy energy as you sit inside your protective shield. Sit in the comfort and protection of this shield for at least five minutes each day.

Journal Prompt: Reflect on the experience of removing or severing unhealthy energy cords. How do you feel after reclaiming your own energy? Do you sense a renewed vitality? What are your concerns about the people whose energy cords you severed? What steps can you take to prevent people from once again implanting energy hooks in you? What does your shield look like? How does it feel to have this protective barrier? Allow yourself to explore any emotions you have about this process.

Once you have taken the necessary steps to remove unhealthy energy, remember to check in with your energy several times throughout the day. By removing unhealthy energy cords, you help to relieve the negative emotions they carry with them, like fear or anger. But, you should also be aware that by removing the hooks that these energy vampires have in you, you might provoke subconscious anger on their part. They might, for example, try to create drama to reconnect with you and get their hooks back in you. If that happens, just remain calm and reinforce your shield by visualizing it vibrating with strong, white light and reflecting their negativity back to them. When they see they will no longer be successful at getting their hooks into you, they'll move on.

You might be wondering how to identify these energy vampires in your life. Well, as we discussed, one way is to check in with how you feel after interacting with different people in your life. The energy vampires will leave you drained, headachy, or even feeling ill. But in addition to this, these are the people who create added drama in your life. They don't take responsibility for their actions, they act like martyrs, they try to make you feel guilty if you don't do what they want, and they tend to diminish your problems while playing up their own. They also try to always 'one-up' you and, if all else fails, they resort to bullying to get their way. In short, they use you for what you give them, but their friendship is a one-way street, where they always receive and you always give. These are energy vampires and, if it is possible, it is always best to avoid having them in your life. If you aren't able to get them out of your life altogether, you can protect yourself using these techniques. When they see they can't take advantage of you anymore, they'll likely move on. Whether they do or not, it's important for you to set appropriate boundaries that meet your needs in a relationship, so let's talk about that some more.

Tip #11—Setting appropriate relationship boundaries: I've already talked about setting boundaries in the context of managing your energy and the work you might do with people in your life around that. But, now we need to talk about setting relationship boundaries and maintaining them for your own good health. As an empath, the emotional connection you have with the people in your life is something you feel more intensely than other people. It's easy to get drawn into the drama in their lives and take it on for yourself. This is particularly true with intimate relationships. But, if you don't take care of yourself, you won't be able to help anyone else. So, how do you set boundaries? Let's start with understanding what it is you want.

1. **Name your limits:** Before you can set boundaries, you have to know what the limits are for each area of your life. The first step to setting boundaries is to identify them. What are your physical, emotional, mental, and spiritual limits? What can you tolerate and accept versus what makes you feel uncomfortable and stressed? In the space below, identify five limits you know you have.

---

1. **Tune into your feelings**: This is key to understanding your limits. Try rating your feelings on a scale of one to ten. Anything that rates a six and above is considered at the higher end. So, when you're having an interaction and you find yourself feeling uncomfortable, rate the level of discomfort and ask yourself what is it that is causing this level of discomfort? Is it what the person is saying or how they're saying it? What is bothering you about the interaction? The feeling of discomfort signals that the other person has crossed

a boundary, but you want to explore exactly why that boundary exists for you.

For example, you might have a fear that you're not a good enough spouse and, during an interaction with your partner, you might begin to feel resentment. It could be that what your partner is saying makes you feel guilty, like you're not doing a good enough job as that person's spouse. Now, once you've identified that's the problem with the interaction, you have to ask yourself a few tough questions. Do you feel what your partner is saying is correct? Is it true? If it is true, does it violate your own expectations for yourself or is it violating the expectations of your partner? If it is violating your own expectations, what can you do to improve the situation so that you live up to what you expect of you? If it is violating the expectations of your partner, but these are not your expectations or values, can you communicate that respectfully to your partner?

Let's take a closer look at this one, because it feeds into the other requirements for setting and maintaining healthy boundaries. Let's say, for example, your partner is upset because you're not spending enough time with them. The first thing to ask is what is the definition of enough time for you and for your partner? If your partner says, "I want you to spend every free moment with me", that's a high expectation on their part, but if they say, "I want a date night every week", that's something you can likely achieve. Once you have identified the expectation for each of you, now you have to realistically assess whether you can meet their needs. As an empath, you likely need a sufficient amount of time alone. Can you get that and fulfill the needs of your partner, as well? If your partner is asking for more than you can give, you have to be prepared to set a firm boundary and be direct in communicating that boundary to them. By opening clear lines of communication, you can understand your needs as well as those of your partner, you can respectfully reach compromises where possible, and you can also respectfully stand firm in your set boundaries, because you will know you are, in fact, a good spouse by exploring their concerns in a thoughtful manner. In the space below, name and rate your five most important needs in an intimate relationship. How much alone time do you need to recharge your batteries? How much time do you feel is important to spend together each day, week, month? What are the most important things you want to get out of a close relationship? Answer those questions and elaborate as needed—go to your journal if you need more space.

---

1. **Give yourself permission:** It's easy to feel guilty for having a need, particularly for the empath. We are taught in our culture to put our own needs aside in favor of others. What you have to realize, however, is that setting boundaries is not just a sign of a healthy relationship, it's also a sign of healthy self-respect. You deserve to feel comfortable and to live your life as you want to live it. **Give yourself permission to set the boundaries you need to feel comfortable, happy, and peaceful in your own life.** In the space below, write out five things you need in your life to feel comfortable, happy, and at peace. For each one of these things, write out a sentence beginning with, "I deserve..." For example, you might write, "I deserve time alone to recharge my battery so I will have energy to do the things I love to do".

1. **Directness:** Maintaining healthy boundaries requires directness. You must communicate clearly to anyone you are in a relationship with what you need in terms of space, time, and styles of communication. Whatever your need, you have to communicate it directly so that there is no misunderstanding. Directness does not mean be rude, rather, you can state your needs in a respectful way. For example, "I love you very much, but I need a lot of time alone. I need at least one hour each day after work to recharge my battery before we do anything together. Allowing me this time will mean I have more positive energy to put into our activities together. That's important to me, because I want you to enjoy being with me as much as I enjoy being with you". Now, practice being direct. In the space below, identify one person with whom you need to set a boundary. Clearly articulate your limit and what you need to improve the relationship. Then, write out a respectful and kind way to let that person know the boundary you are setting. State it directly, but respectfully—if you need more space, go to your journal.

1. **Make self-care a priority:** Particularly for empaths, the reality is that if you're unhappy, the other people in your life will be unhappy, as well. You not only have the ability to receive and feel their emotions, you have the ability to forcefully project your own emotions outward. That's why you have to make your own needs a priority. That doesn't mean you don't compromise in your close relationships, but it does mean that your priority must be with taking care of yourself. You need to be aware of and honor your feelings and needs. By taking

care of yourself, you will ensure you have the energy to help your loved ones when they need you. You'll be a better friend, spouse, parent, and coworker if you ensure your needs are met. In the space below, list five ways you can improve on your self-care and write out a plan for doing just that. For example, you might list practicing morning meditation and your plan for implementing that could begin with 15 minutes of meditation each morning.

By practicing these boundary setting exercises, you'll be better able to identify your needs and where you might need to set better boundaries in order to take good care of yourself. But, sometimes you engage in toxic relationships and this is an area of particular vulnerability for the empath.

The Empath and Toxic Relationships

If you practice good self-care and are aware of and responsive to your own needs, you'll likely avoid engaging in toxic relationships, but empaths are particularly susceptible to this, because they feel emotional energy so intensely. To identify if you're in a toxic relationship of any kind, ask yourself the following questions:

- How do I feel in the company of that person?
- Am I my authentic self when I'm around that person?
- How does it feel when I leave their company?
- Do they make me feel creative and inspired?
- Do they make me feel supported?

If your answers to these questions are negative—you don't feel positively when you're in their company, you're not authentic self, you feel much better when you leave their company, they don't inspire you to be better or act on your creative ideas, and you don't feel supported in their presence—this is likely a toxic relationship. It's a one-way street and you're always going against traffic. Because of their giving and sensitive nature, most empaths are engaged in at least one toxic relationship. They want to help others heal and they can see the good in everyone, but that means it is sometimes easy for other people to take advantage of their kind nature. So, how can you say goodbye when you're in a toxic relationship?

Because the empath is so sensitive to emotional energy, it's hard for them to let go suddenly. That's why it is often better to slowly retract using a process rather than simply cutting the cord at one time. The process starts with distancing yourself from the person. This can take two to three weeks to do effectively. Begin with small steps. For example, if you eat lunch together every day, then make it every other day. By slowly adjusting your time together, you both are able to establish new routines. Then, begin enjoying time with those people who fill you up with positive emotions. You will be feeling two sets of pain when you disengage from this toxic relationship and so you'll need strong emotional support. Call in the backup and make sure you take extra time for self-care. The last step is to formulate a plan for ending the relationship. Not every relationship will end in the same way. A coworker is different from a lover or a family member. Sometimes the relationship can't end entirely (as with a family member, for example), but you can set new and strict boundaries on when and how you interact. Whatever the plan is, make sure it is something you can carry out and remember that you must stick it out if you are going to truly take care of yourself. You are deserving of every good thing in your life and you have a right to take the necessary steps to ensure your happiness and peace of mind. **I would very much appreciate your thoughts about my book and your feedback means a LOT to me.**

The Underestimated Challenges Empaths Face And How To Overcome Them

To maintain a high level of physical and mental energy, it is extremely important for the empath to take care of themselves. Because of their increased sensitivity, empaths often underestimate certain challenges that plague everyone, but impact the empath in a particularly severe manner. I know there were times in my life when I was guilty of underestimating these challenges and I had to make some changes to improve my energy flow. It cannot be understated that protecting and cultivating energy is important for the empath. So, let's look at some of the challenges that can compromise your energy as an empath and you can overcome them:

- **Physical and Mental Fatigue:** This is a huge problem for the empath who is so connected to everyone else's energy that they sometimes fail to recognize deficits in their own energy. That's why it is extremely important for the empath to get sufficient sleep and reduce stress. We talked about how the sympathetic nervous system is also known as the fight or flight nervous system. It gears you up for the fight or the flight, but in doing so, it secretes hormones like adrenaline and cortisol and these can negatively impact your health. Additionally, because your brain sees any kind of fear as requiring the activation of this system, even those non-life threatening fears like, "I'm afraid I'll lose my job" or "I'm afraid my car will break down", cause the activation of this system. This results in adrenal fatigue and can affect your sleep patterns, as well as your general sense of wellbeing. What can you do?

First, learn how to stimulate your parasympathetic nervous system—that's the one that calms you down. There are a number of scientifically proven ways to activate your vagus nerve, which is effectively the heart of the parasympathetic nervous system. These include meditation that uses chanting, deep breathing techniques that expand your belly as you inhale, massage therapy, and even singing in the shower. When the vagus nerve is activated, the parasympathetic nervous system activates hormonal responses that help calm you down and leave you with peaceful, good feelings.

Tip #12—Chanting meditation: Try this technique to utilize several ways at once to activate the vagus nerve and your parasympathetic nervous system. Do this meditative technique every morning and, when you are faced with a crisis, do an abbreviated version for just a few minutes to help keep you calm:

a. Sit in a comfortable, but alert position and close your eyes;
b. Focus on your breath—take deep breaths, inhaling the air and expanding both your belly and your chest as you do. Do this for 10 inhale/exhale breathing cycles.
c. Begin chanting 'Om'. Try extending the 'Om' sound so that you can feel your vocal cords vibrating. The vagus nerve innervates your vocal cords and doing this activates the nerve. Continue chanting for several minutes.
d. Visualize yourself in a peaceful place of your choosing. Let yourself feel the tranquility and the calmness of this place. Feel the calm energy entering your body, filling you up and charging your batteries.
e. Express gratitude for this time you've taken for yourself and let that feeling of gratitude infuse your entire body. Now, send it

out to the universe.
f. Focus again on your breath. Repeat 10 inhale/exhale cycles of breathing expanding into your belly. When you're ready, open your eyes.

If you're experiencing insomnia related to this physical and mental fatigue, try this meditation technique before bed in the evening. You can use an abbreviated version of deep breathing and visualizing your peaceful place when you find you're triggered during the day.

- **Physical Health**: When you get caught up in the emotional energies around you, it is easy to forget to take good care of your physical energy. We're talking about diet and exercise here, but let's look at a few specific tips for the empath.

Tip #13—Dietary choices: Because you're energetically attuned to other people, animals, plants, and the environment, you'll want to make choices that show respect and compassion for life as a whole. The best choices will nourish your body and your soul. When deciding what to eat, you might ask yourself the following questions:

a. Is this food produced in a healthy way that nourishes my body without introducing unwanted chemicals?
b. Is this food produced in a manner that is consistent with my values?
c. Am I providing my body with the necessary nutrients to keep it healthy?
d. Does the way I eat show respect and compassion for my health and my body?

If the answers to those questions cause you to feel bad in any way, you might want to consider making better choices. You'll also want to make choices that best nourish your body. You'll want to reduce your intake of refined sugar and starchy foods. Does that mean you can never eat these things? No, but everything in moderation is a good rule and, if you have specific health problems, you might need to eliminate certain additives, like salt if you have high blood pressure. This might seem like a huge ask, but the reality is when you reduce your intake of harmful foods, you'll start to feel so much better that you'll know it was worth the sacrifice and, eventually, it won't feel like a sacrifice at all.

Tip #14—Exercise: Exercise is extremely important for the empath because it is one way to release built up emotional energy. Of course, you have to choose an exercise regimen that is right for your level of fitness and any health challenges you have, but it's also important to choose an exercise program that resonates with your sensitivities. For example, dance routines can help to express and expel the emotional energy you've built up and they provide a way for you to express yourself artistically. So, think about what kind of movement resonates with you. Is it dancing or running or yoga? Any of these can be helpful for discharging that absorbed energy and—bonus—exercise, like yoga, also stimulates the vagus nerve and your parasympathetic nervous system. If you're just starting out, take it slow and build up in a healthy way.

- **Mental Health**: This is extremely important for the empath because of the absorbed energies they take on. You really have to take care of your mental health. I've discussed several strategies to employ to help you offload absorbed emotional energy and I've talked about the importance of setting boundaries. You should use these techniques regularly, but you also need to do things that you enjoy and that help to relax you.

***Tip #15: Relaxing activities*--**This might include getting out into nature on a regular basis, planning some alone time, processing your emotions with a good friend, or creating real or imagined distance where needed. This could also include activities that allow you to express your artistic side.

***Tip #16: Seek Professional Help if Needed*—**It's also important to note that there is no shame in getting professional help when you feel you can no longer effectively help yourself. A professional can lend an objective ear where a friend is biased on your behalf. Taking care of yourself is of paramount importance and, because of your sensitive nature, it is easy to suffer emotional angst. If you're going to help anyone else in your life, you must first help yourself.

These strategies will help you to overcome these often underestimated challenges that can forcefully impact an empath. By practicing good self-care, you'll find your own energy will soar.

The Mystical Way: The Empath And Spirituality

It's often easy to feel overwhelmed as an empath. I have felt this way myself and I know it can be easy to feel like this gift is a burden, but the reality is that becoming empathic is part of the process for spiritual awakening. Part of spiritual awakening involves a shift in consciousness that makes anyone more empathic and for those who are already an empath, that shift in consciousness can bring an increased sense of being overwhelmed. This is another reason it's important to understand how to manage those energetic sensations you're feeling. But, before I address this further, let's look at a few signs that indicate you are undergoing a powerful spiritual awakening:

- One big indicator of a spiritual awakening is that what you feel is something that is impossible to put into words. You feel different, but the feeling is so distinct that you can't explain it. It's as if the world was in black and white before and now it's in vivid color. It even has a new taste, but really what's changed is the eyes through which you're looking at the world. Suddenly, you see what's real and what's an illusion.

- You also see what has been negative in your life. You realize what represents the old you and you know that you don't want to do these negative or destructive things anymore. You're ready for something new and you want nothing but good for yourself and everyone else.

- You might also feel the need to seek out other people who are also experiencing their own awakening. Just like with anything else in your life, it helps to have people who get where you're coming from and that's just as true with a spiritual awakening. Many people who are currently in your life might not understand what you're going through and you might, therefore, find yourself seeking out those who will understand.

- You might also find that you now avoid anything superficial and people or things who are not authentic. When you plug into what is real, it's very hard to continue with those things that are distractions or superficial. You might find that you avoid people, places, and activities that don't express the authenticity you're now experiencing for yourself. It's easy to view this as antisocial, but it's simply a healthy sign that you are tuning in to the universal soul.

- You are also quite likely to feel a deep compassion for all entities. You'll be more highly attuned to both the joy and the suffering in the world and you'll experience these feelings very deeply. It can even cause depression if you don't know how to process what you're experiencing.

- You will also likely experience a need to make the world a better place and to have a positive impact on those around you. You might not know how to best accomplish this, but if you keep yourself open and grounded, the way will be revealed to you.

As you grapple with the immensity of a spiritual awakening, there are a number of things you can do to help you grow in this experience. Let's examine a few techniques that can help you to grow into this new reality.

*Tip #17—**Journaling***: I know I probably sound like a broken record, but expressing your feelings is one of the best ways to process your spiritual awakening, particularly for empaths. One of the things I have experienced is a feeling that I'm not doing my spiritual awakening correctly. I think that's a common feeling, particularly if you don't suddenly find yourself free from all negative emotions, floating on air like a saint. But, as I processed my experiences through journaling, I came to see that it's not about not feeling negative emotions, it's about feeling everything and then letting those feelings pass through you, while you stay grounded in the present moment.

*Tip #18—**Stay grounded***: To say stay in the present moment seems easy, but it's more complicated than it seems. When the present moment is something mystical and joyful, it's easy to stay there, but when it's frustrating or frightening, well that's a horse of a different color. What I have to come to understand through my experience is that the point of being in the present moment is precisely to feel everything in that moment, to live it fully. So, how do you process it? You have to let the feelings flow through you without grabbing onto them and the story your ego wants to create around them. For example, if something frustrating is happening, your ego might start whispering in your ear, "You're not good enough. You need to get angry. You need to let them know who you are". But, that's just your ego trying to tell you a story and it wants you to believe that story. Once you recognize that and call it out, you get it out of the way so that you can let go of the feelings you're experiencing.

*Tip #19—**Sit with your feelings***: You have to let go of any story your ego wants to tell you in order for the feelings you're experiencing to be able to flow through you. But, you also have to be willing to actually experience those feelings. That's hard when they're negative. To sit with these more difficult feelings, try getting someplace where you can express these feelings freely and simply let yourself feel them. Whether it involves anger or sadness, let them flow freely. As they do, notice how it feels in your body. Where do you experience the anger in your body? Where do you experience the sadness in your body? Let yourself cry or yell or curse. This is part of fully experiencing the richness of life in all of its emotional expressions. Once you sit with these feelings and notice their effect on you, you will also notice as they simply move on and you will feel better.

Tip #20—Understand core beliefs: This is another part of processing the intense feelings you're likely to experience with a spiritual awakening. Almost everyone accepts some negative core beliefs about themselves as they grow up and get beat up by life. When you're experiencing something like anger or shame, you want to get at the core belief behind your emotional reaction. This is an exercise we discussed before, but it's a very effective one. Turn around and see your little self-feeling angry or hurt or ashamed and ask him or her why they feel that way. Now, listen to the answer and then provide them with the comfort that little you should have received the moment the core belief was adopted. Let's take an example to explain this more.

Perhaps that little you did something you shouldn't have done—haven't we all? Maybe you got in trouble and maybe in a moment of frustration, a parent or guardian said something like, "How could you be so stupid?" At that point, that little you might well have adopted the core belief, "I am stupid". So, when you find yourself in another situation later in life where you're feeling ashamed, your little you might say, "I feel bad because I'm so stupid". Now is your chance to heal that old wound. Tell that little you, "I understand why you feel that way. Your mother asked how you could be so stupid and now you think that's true. But, you know what I know about you? I know you're a survivor and even though you sometimes make mistakes, that doesn't mean you're stupid. It means you're human and I love you, even when you do something wrong". That's the message you should have gotten, but everyone makes mistakes, including the parent or guardian who might have told you something like that. Being your own hero will help heal your old wound and bring the light of compassion to yourself and those who might have harmed you. By practicing this exercise, you'll find you can heal many of your old wounds.

Journal Prompt: Now, it's time for you to practice the exercise above. Think of a time when you felt angry or ashamed and take yourself through the process of understanding the core belief behind your feelings. What did you come to believe about yourself? Can you take yourself back to the moment where you formed your core belief and allow yourself to see the entire context of what occurred? Can you understand why you did the things you did? Even if now you think that what you did wasn't smart, can you understand why that younger you did the best he or she could in the moment? Can you have compassion for your younger self? Can you have compassion for any of the other people involved? Can you see their struggles? Let yourself feel any emotions that arise and notice what is the story attached to the emotion. Can you sit with these emotions and allow them to work their way out of your body? Let them flow and bless them on their way. Write about this experience in your journal. Document the context and what happened and bring the light of love and compassion to yourself and the others involved in the situation.

Engaging in this process will allow you to accept and even love your shadow self. Your shadow self is that part of yourself that you're ashamed of—you might perceive it as weak or angry or bad. It's not any of these things, however, it's just a part of yourself that has a role in your survival and coping abilities. By bringing your shadow self into the light of your self-compassion, you will give this part of you the love it needs, so you can fully accept yourself and everything that is part of you.

This is critical for your spiritual growth and awakening. If you don't fully accept and love yourself, you might have a tendency to engage in spiritual bypassing. This is where you use your spirituality as an excuse to avoid confronting unresolved emotional issues. You might think, for example, "This is just how I am and everything is perfect as it is, therefore, I don't need to do anything about it". This is a trap, because by not confronting your unresolved issues, they will continue to hinder your spiritual growth.

You might be wondering why this is particularly important. If you don't deal with your own stuff, it will make you much more vulnerable to psychic attacks from other empaths. Knowing what are truly your emotions through processing them will help you understand when you are receiving and experiencing the emotions of other people. When someone in a negative mindset projects their energies your way, you can experience a toxic reaction to these low frequency energetic emissions if you don't know how to process and identify your own energies as distinct from those of other people.

*Tip #21—***Fend off psychic attacks**: So when you find yourself thinking repetitive negative thoughts, stop and process those emotions to determine whether or not they belong to you. If you find they are the product of a psychic attack—that is to say they are coming from someone else—practice the techniques I've discussed to both discharge that negative energy and transform it into a positive emotion. Then, you can project that positive emotion out to the world, including to the one who might be attacking you. Be sure to put up your protective shield after doing these rituals. This will help to prevent them from attacking you again.

*Tip #22—***Understand the different energies**: Understanding the energy around you is also key to both protecting yourself and helping others to heal. It starts with understanding how energy moves through your own body. Your aura is an electromagnetic field that extends from your core to around four or five feet around your body. It's simply your energy field. Like an onion, there are layers to your aura. These layers are defined as the following and they correspond to your chakras:

- The *Etheric* Body – This is the first layer, which resonates at 20 cycles per minute and spreads out up to two inches beyond your physical self. This layer holds information about your physical health.

- The *Emotional* Body – The second layer, which extends to one to three inches from the physical body, contains your feelings.

- The *Mental* Body – The third layer, which extends to between three and eight inches from the body, contains your ideas, thoughts, and mental processes.

- The *Astral* Level – The fourth layer, which extends to about a foot from the body, represents the bridge to the spiritual realm and the astral plane.

- The *Etheric* Template Body – The fifth layer, which extends to about a foot and a half from the body, is thought to coexist on a different dimension. It is typically only visible to healers and clairvoyants.

- The *Celestial* Body – The sixth layer is where communication with the spiritual realm takes place and it is where you experience ecstasy and unconditional love. This is the layer involved in heightened levels of consciousness.

- The *Causal* Body or Ketheric Template – The seventh layer extends three to five feet from the body and it contains all of the other bodies. This is a reflection of everything your soul has undergone and it vibrates with God energy. This is the link to the Divine, where you accept your oneness with the universe.

Each auric layer has seven chakras and they all communicate with each other and exchange energy. That's why it's imperative to keep your energy flowing freely. These auric layers are the source of your Kundalini energy—your life force energy. As you experience a spiritual awakening, you are really experiencing a Kundalini awakening. It is the realization of the oneness of all energy and it can be very traumatic. You might experience a number of different sensations. But, never fear, there are several ways to deal with the incoming energy.

It's helpful as you connect to these different energies that you stay in tune with your psycho-energetic centers, known as chakras. There are six chakras and a seventh center, all of which can help you understand the different levels of consciousness. If one or more of them become blocked, then it will result in feelings of discomfort, disharmony, stress and even illness. These chakras all communicate with the auric chakras. The six chakras are the following:

- *Muladhara*—The root chakra at the base of your spine; this is probably the most practical of the chakras and is more concerned with grounding and balance than purely with the realms of the spirit. This is where the lower body and the chakras meet, and it is very often considered the foundation of physical wellbeing. It helps us balance, maintain stability and generally keep things together. When it is blocked, our whole equilibrium seems to be disrupted and this can affect everything from our work to how we carry ourselves and even how we perceive ourselves physically.

- *Svadhisthana*—the sacral chakra at the third vertebra of the sacrum; it is associated with sexual activity and also with other things like money, creativity, joy, and intimacy. When working optimally, we feel creative, self-aware, positive and successful. People whose sacral chakras are working well seem to be bursting with energy and self-confidence. Once blocked, it is, of course, a very different story. You immediately start to feel off-balance, unmotivated and uninspired. Without that motivation, it is difficult to lift oneself from the rut that you will have fallen into. You will not want to do much and even your sex drive will wither away.

- *Manipura*—the navel chakra at the level of the navel on the spine; often referred to as the solar plexus. It regulates the function of the pancreas and digestive organs. When it is blocked, you will feel a loss of appetite, body shakes, palpitations increase, low self-esteem, fatigue and anxiety.

- *Anahata*—the heart chakra at mid-chest level; it is the point where the physical and spiritual merge and it is the foundation of our positive emotional wellbeing. It affects the health of our heart, lungs, chest, arms and thymus gland. When it is blocked, we are susceptible to feelings of contempt, scorn, and even hate.

- *Vishuddha*—the throat chakra, located just above the hollow of the neck; there are two signs for the empath that the throat chakra has become blocked. Either you will have trouble speaking at all, or you will speak too much and often say things that are an exaggeration or are false. In general, these will be things that make you look better in the eyes of others. The reason for this is that the lack of confidence that many empaths live with tend to make them overcompensate in one way or another. They either want to shrink away and hide from the world, or they want to portray an image of self-confidence. In a way, both of these symptoms are a way of hiding one's true self. When this chakra is blocked, you may notice physical indicators such as a sore throat, thyroid problems or neck pain.

- *Ajna*—the third eye chakra, located in the center of the brain and accessed through the middle of the forehead; it plays a dominant role in your intuitive abilities and clear-headed thinking. It also promotes a clear focus. When it is blocked, this leads to depression, dizzy spells, poor memory and recall, and headaches. More noticeable, perhaps, will be your sudden loss in confidence in your inner voice. Clearing the blocked third eye chakra involves sitting comfortably but upright with the eyes closed. Breathe deeply and then start to focus your mind on that point between your eyebrows. Next, imagine a purple light being focused on that point. Keep focusing on this as well as your breathing until you sense some relief.

The seventh center is not really considered a chakra, because it is the portal towards oneness. It is known as **Sahasrara** and it is referred to as the crown chakra, located at the top of your head. It promotes awareness, social consciousness, and brings feelings of serenity and deep peace of life. When it is blocked or fails to function properly, then you can experience a sense of being isolated from others, even when you are in a crowd. You might even be distressed and depressed so easily.

To connect to these energies, it is helpful to envision them as whorling vortices of bright light connecting one to the other. Allow yourself to envision that energy rising from the root chakra up through each successive center until it pours out of Sahasrara, as you connect to the universal oneness. This is your birthright.

*Tip #23—**Dealing with positive feelings***: The truth is that even positive feelings can be overwhelming. With a Kundalini awakening, you might experience bliss, grandiose feelings, and heart openings where you feel love for everyone. The key to dealing with these types of emotions is to seek grounding tools and set healthy boundaries. It's fine to enjoy the good feelings but ground yourself in the present moment and the understanding that nothing is forever. When these intense good feelings pass, you'll still be grounded and on the right path.

*Tip #24—**Psychic experiences***: These experiences might happen from time to time, because as you awaken, the strength of your psychic connections increases and you're easily able to traverse time. You can sit with the experiences and even enjoy them, but don't become too attached to anything you experience, since these sensations, like everything, are temporary. Also, be sure to process the emotions that arise. It might also help to make use of oracle cards. These can help you to navigate the energetically charged world around you. These cards can help you and your loved ones, as well.

*Tip #25—**Dealing with constant insights and energetic flows***: As an empath, you'll experience the energetic flows intensely and the insights will just keep coming. Write down the insights, because you're having them for a reason and they will be useful. For energetic flow, practice the techniques I've discussed to discharge negative energies and transform them into positive emotions.

*Tip #26—**Dealing with negative emotions***: Since you'll be more open to emotional energy, you're likely to experience negative emotions, too. These could include fear, anxiety, sadness, and even terror. You could even have a panic attack. Remember to use the techniques we discussed to activate your vagus nerve and the parasympathetic nervous system. Those methods will help calm you down. Remember to stay grounded in the present moment and use the methods we talked about to process the energy.

*Tip #27—**Collective pain***: As you open to the connectedness of all things, you might experience the collective pain of many in despair. These sensations will pass, but it is a good idea to use a meditation practice to understand what the lesson is in these sensations. Is there something you can do to help, even if it is a small contribution?

*Tip #28—**Vivid, lucid dreams***: Lucid dreams are the kind where you physically experience the dream. You should be particularly aware of these and write them down in your journal. It's recommended that you write them down immediately upon waking. These dreams often contain messages important to your awakening experience. Reflect on the significance of any symbolism for your life and your awakened experience.

*Tip #29—**Physical sensations***: You might experience a number of different kinds of physical sensations. These could include heat at the bottom of your spine, weight loss, weight gain, digestive issues, pressure or pain in random places, skin conditions, and autoimmune problems. It is very important to maintain a healthy diet and exercise routine in order to minimize these symptoms. It can also help to practice energy enhancing exercises, like yoga and/or get a relaxing massage.

Tip #30—Sleep disturbances: The intensity of the energy you're perceiving can certainly affect your sleep patterns. Here is where a good relaxing meditation practice will come in handy. Try the following—it has helped me on many a sleepless night:

- Lay down in a comfortable position and close your eyes;

- Focus your breath and go through 10 deep breathing inhalation/exhalation cycles;

- Become aware of your body—feel how your arms and legs feel on the bed;

- Beginning at your head, intentionally relax the muscles of your head and face, followed by your neck, then go down your body to your shoulders, arms, and chest. Notice the sensation of the muscles relaxing and the parts of your body sinking into the bed. Breathe deeply as you do this process. Now, continue down into your abdomen and legs. Let your limbs settle into a relaxed position.

- Now, turn your attention to the sounds you can hear. Separate out the sounds you hear in the background. How many do you hear? Can you hear insects in the background—crickets or cicadas? Can you hear the wind or the rain?

- Let yourself focus in on one soothing sound—perhaps the wind or the rain. Let your breathing normalize in rhythm and depth.

- Finally, let your mind drift off to sleep as you express gratitude for the quiet moments of life.

Tip #31—Dealing with overstimulation: Overstimulation is a common problem for empaths. If you are dealing with this problem, it can help to avoid large crowds, make use of noise cancellation headphones, and make time to spend in nature. This will all help deal with overstimulation.

Tip #32—Feeling overwhelmed: With all of this stimulation, it's normal to feel overwhelmed. To deal with this, you want to take a step back, focus on one thing at a time, and be gentle with yourself. Meditation and walks in nature can help to relieve feeling overwhelmed.

Tip #33—Changes in mood: You might experience sudden shifts in mood, from extreme joy and bliss to sadness or fear. Remember to sit with your feelings and process them to ensure they are indeed your emotions and not projections from someone nearby. Discharge negative energies and stay grounded in the present moment with the understanding that emotions are temporary and will pass.

Tip #34—Feeling fragmented: Because of the variety of energies you're sensing, you might feel fragmented. Using some of the meditation techniques I've discussed can help to reestablish your sense of connectedness with the universal soul.

Tip #35—Extreme sensitivity to content: You might become very sensitive to the content in various media, like the news or social media. It might be necessary to avoid these media while you practice grounding techniques to relieve your sensitivity.

The tips I've discussed here will help you to fully explore your spirituality and experience the benefits of an awakening. Remember that the richness of life is the reason we came into this form to experience. That richness includes all of the various emotions we feel, as well as the physical sensations and personal growth. We experience life and learn various coping skills and, then, if we're lucky enough to experience an empathic awakening, we remember the oneness from which we came and we can learn to help ourselves and others heal. But, we must understand how to handle the difficulties that we will still experience, even as awakened beings.

Essential Tools and Techniques Every Empath Should Know

It's important for empaths to understand the tools you have at your disposal to help soothe your overstimulated body, mind, and soul. I've spoken at length about grounding yourself and there are various tools you can use for this purpose. Let's discuss some of the methods you can easily employ:

Tip #36—Take a cold shower: This might not sound very soothing, but it stimulates your vagus nerve and activates your parasympathetic nervous system. That will help to keep you calm and grounded.

Tip #37—Massage: Massage is a great relaxation technique and massaging certain pressure points on the body stimulates the vagus nerve and, therefore, the parasympathetic nervous system. It also helps keep energy moving through the body.

Tip #38—Spend time with animals: Animals are a great way to reduce your blood pressure and calm your mind. They are always grounded in the present moment and they can help keep you grounded, too.

Tip #39—Reiki: Reiki is a form of alternative medicine that is referred to as energy healing. It became known in Japan in the late 1800s and it involves the transfer of energy from the practitioner to the patient. Like Traditional Chinese Medicine techniques, the aim of the therapy is to help reestablish the flow of the body's energy. It is believed that illness is the result of stagnated energy. The practice of reiki is believed to unblock stagnated energy, much in the same way that acupuncture or acupressure does. It can help you to reestablish a healthy flow of energy and it's a relaxing technique.

Tip #40—Music: Listening to music allows you to process your feelings in a conscious way. It deeply shifts the energy and emotions you feel and singing along stimulates the vagus nerve and, as a result, the parasympathetic nervous system.

Tip #41—Harness crystal energy: Crystals can offer you healing energy and by spending time in a crystal store, you'll feel the stones calling to you. When you feel ungrounded, use a stone to help you reestablish your sense of calm.

Tip #42—Visualizations: I've discussed the power of visualizations and they can also be used to ground you. You can use visualizations to shield yourself from unwanted energies and you can infuse yourself with the healing power of white light.

Tip #43—Affirmations: There's real scientific evidence supporting the benefits of positive affirmations (Critcher & Dunning, 2014). It's a quick way to ground yourself, especially when you're feeling overwhelmed by life. A few good affirmations include the following:

- I am one with all that is and I am one with the earth and my body.

- I am connected to Source at all times and it replenishes me constantly.

- I am like a tree—deeply rooted and grounded in the One, but flexible to the winds of life.

Remind yourself of these realities frequently. Use these affirmations or make some of your own.

Tip #44—Laughter: It's true what they say about laughter being the best medicine. A good belly laugh activates your vagus nerve and parasympathetic nervous system. So, watch a few comedians you like or a funny movie and let yourself laugh—it's good for you.

Tip #45—Chanting: Chanting, like singing, will also activate your vagus nerve and parasympathetic nervous system. A great practice is called **Kirtan Kriya**. The chant involves repetitions of the following mantra: **Sa Ta Na Ma**. Each part means the following:

- SA which is birth, the beginning, the infinity, and the totality;
- TA is life, existence, and creativity;
- NA is death, change, and transformation;
- MA is rebirth, regeneration, and resurrection.

There's even scientific evidence (Marciniak et al., 2014) that demonstrates the health benefits of chanting.

Tip #46—Smudging: Smudging is sometimes referred to as sagging. It involves burning herbs in a room or home to remove bad energy and help carry one's dreams to the universe. Smudging with sacred smoke has magical properties and benefits. It can clear away any unwanted energy in your physical space and it also clears out your mental and emotional space.

Tip #47—Essential oils: The scents of essential oils can help you feel grounded with just a few quick inhales. There are three great oils for this purpose and you should carry a scent with you everywhere you go. Just place a few drops in your palms, rub your hands together, and inhale until you once again feel grounded. The three oils that work well for this are:

- Prime Natural Anxiety Relief Blend
- DoTerra's Grounding Blend
- Young Living's Grounding Essential Oil

Tip #48—Practice Tai Chi: Grounding is at the heart of the practice of Tai Chi. The practice is about establishing a deeper connection to the ground. Practicing these ancient exercises helps you bring harmony and balance into your life.

Tip #49—Get enough sleep: The benefits of enough sleep cannot be underestimated and it's worth mentioning again. Sleep helps cleanse your mind and refresh your body. Make getting enough sleep a priority in your life.

By using these tools, you can maintain a healthy, harmonious balance in your life and you can better manage your energy. This will allow you to help yourself and others manage and control the various energies of life and it will help you overcome many of life's challenges.

The Last Tip Empaths Should Never Forget

This last tip is perhaps the most important one for the empath. It's so easy to get caught up in life, particularly since, as an empath, you are exposed to so many energetic forces. You have a gift, but to use it properly, you have to stay healthy and maintain a constant control over the energies you perceive. You have to know how to discharge negative energy and how to transform it into positive energy. You have to know how to ground yourself and how to deal with the challenges of the spiritual awakening that almost always accompanies empathic abilities. You are a spiritual being, an energetic force of nature, and your gift can help you and everyone around you to live a fuller, richer life.

I've talked about several tips for effectively managing your energy and the energetic forces that you perceive. Meditation and journaling will help you process your feelings and recognize your own emotions versus those of others around you. Chanting, singing, and deep breathing will help to activate your vagus nerve and, therefore, your parasympathetic nervous system. Smudging can help you clear your physical, mental, and emotional space and essential oils can help you ground yourself on a moment's notice. Physical exercise will help keep your physical energy high and eating right will keep you healthy and properly fuel your body. For the empath, these practices and the many more I've discussed are particularly important. But, there is one last tip that the empath should never forget.

Tip #50—Play: You came to this physical form to experience the richness of life in all its variety. You came to experience joy, sadness, triumph, failure, anger, peace, and all of the other emotional and physical sensations that life brings. So, live it, feel it, and don't forget to enjoy it. Go out and play—play like you did when you were a little kid. Children are much closer to the universal One because life hasn't gotten in their way yet. They play and imagine and do all the things that bring them joy. No matter what age you are, playing never gets old. Go out and make snow angels, skip through the park, lay on the grass and watch the clouds go by, play fetch with your best friend, and live life to its fullest. Play, live, love, and enjoy this life you came to experience. Stay grounded in the present moment—something playing can help you do. It brings you into the joy of the moment and focuses your attention on the sensations that bring you happiness. Empaths have some of the richest lives out there because they genuinely feel all emotions so intensely. We are lucky for that and we deserve a rich life full of play!

Taking this journey alone is not recommended so I highly encourage you to join our friendly community on Facebook to maximize the value you receive from this book. What often helps a lot is connecting with other like-minded empaths. People you can relate to, get support from and learn from on how to navigate this world with your unique gift. This can be an excellent support network for you.

It would be great to connect with you there,

Alison L. Alverson

To join, visit: www.facebook.com/groups/empathsupportcommunity/[1]

---

1. http://www.facebook.com/groups/empathsupportcommunity/

Finally, thank you again for grabbing my book! Your opinion matters! Please share your thoughts about my book on the platform you bought from, and don't be shy, the more information, the better.

Thank you and good luck!

A Bonus Chapter Of My Book:
CHAKRA HEALING FOR BEGINNERS

The Complete Guide to Awaken and Balance Chakras for Self-Healing and Positive Energy

Alison L. Alverson

© **Copyright 2020 by Alison L. Alverson - All rights reserved.**

This document is geared towards providing exact and reliable information in regards to the topic and issue covered. The publication is sold with the idea that the publisher is not required to render an accounting, officially permitted, or otherwise, qualified services. If advice is necessary, legal or professional, a practiced individual in the profession should be ordered.

- From a Declaration of Principles which was accepted and approved equally by a Committee of the American Bar Association and a Committee of Publishers and Associations.

In no way is it legal to reproduce, duplicate, or transmit any part of this document in either electronic means or in printed format. Recording of this publication is strictly prohibited and any storage of this document is not allowed unless with written permission from the publisher. All rights reserved.

The information provided herein is stated to be truthful and consistent, in that any liability, in terms of inattention or otherwise, by any usage or abuse of any policies, processes, or directions contained within is the solitary and utter responsibility of the recipient reader. Under no circumstances will any legal responsibility or blame be held against the publisher for any reparation, damages, or monetary loss due to the information herein, either directly or indirectly.

Respective authors own all copyrights not held by the publisher.

The information herein is offered for informational purposes solely and is universal as so. The presentation of the information is without a contract or any type of guarantee assurance.

The trademarks that are used are without any consent, and the publication of the trademark is without permission or backing by the trademark owner. All trademarks and brands within this book are for clarifying purposes only and are owned by the owners themselves, not affiliated with this document

Energizing Your Chakras Through Guided Meditation

Meditation is a great way to energize your chakras, but meditation can be daunting if you're a beginner, and you may even have developed a strong resistance to it. That's where guided meditation can help. There are many apps and online websites that provide guided meditation, but there are still several mistakes you'll want to avoid, even with this kind of help. Some of the more common errors include things like falling asleep, finding it difficult to stay focused, failing to prepare your meditation environment properly, trying to force yourself to meditate, not setting a consistent time for meditation, setting your expectations too high, and/or having difficulty establishing a daily routine. So, what are the best ways to avoid these mistakes?

Before we get into avoiding your mistakes, it's helpful to understand the effect of unbalanced chakras. As discussed earlier, each chakra is associated with various organs, illnesses, and symptoms like fatigue. Unbalanced chakras are particularly problematic for the empath. Empaths are already vulnerable from the effects of too much emotional energy bombarding them, and unbalanced chakras can make that situation even worse. Unbalanced chakras can result in leaky auras that further drains the empath and lets in even more unwanted energy from the people they contact.

Unbalanced chakras, in general, can make all parts of your life very difficult. You'll feel ungrounded and unhappy. This creates more stress, which harms the health of your chakras. They are also affected by personal trauma and anxiety. They can be forced permanently open by regularly using chemical drugs, medications, a poor diet, and excessive alcohol use or smoking. Treating the imbalances is imperative for your health, given that the chakras are like energetic glands. When they're in balance, they 'secrete' the necessary energy to maintain both physical and mental health, which means they work to keep your physical endocrine system in balance.

Balancing the chakras is achieved through spiritual healing and meditative practices. That's easy to say, but sometimes challenging to do. Let's look at the common mistakes and how you can avoid them so that your meditative experience will genuinely help heal any chakra imbalances or blockages.

1. **Meditation Is Not Mandatory**

When you think of anything as something you have to do, it is almost guaranteed to kill your desire and motivation to do it. While meditation is essential to keeping your chakras working correctly, there are other things you can do. Here is a quick list of other ways to help balance and maintain your chakras' health:

- **Spend time in nature:** Being out in nature helps you feel more connected to the universe's healing energy. It keeps you grounded and cultivates a peaceful feeling.

- **Creative visualization:** By visualizing those things that make you feel happy and satisfied, you bring balance and harmony to your chakras' functioning. It can be something as simple as visualizing a flower opening, or it can be more complex, such as visualizing your perfect life as if you already are living it.

- **Breathe deeply:** Breathing with intention is an effective way to restore your chakras. You will bring them into their natural, harmonic balance. You breathe with intention by inhaling energy into your chakra and then exhaling as awareness settles into the chakra.

- **Wearing the right colors:** Each color represents a specific vibration. If you're wearing the proper color for a particular chakra, you can help heal any blockages or imbalances in that chakra. The chakra colors include red for your root chakra, orange for the sacral chakra, yellow for the solar plexus, green or pink for the heart, blue for the throat, indigo or purple for the third eye, and purple or white for the crown chakra.

- **Practice gratitude:** Whenever you express gratitude, you instantly raise your vibrational frequency, and that acts to open your chakras and attract more positive things into your life.

2. You're Actively Trying to Stop Your Thoughts

This is a common reason why people resist meditation. The truth is that meditation isn't about stopping your thoughts; instead, it's about noticing your thoughts and then letting them go. Don't fight your wandering mind, but notice when it does wander and what your thoughts are like. Are you planning what you'll eat for dinner? Are you worried about a loved one? Do you remember an earlier time in your life? Rather than trying to stop those thoughts from coming, if you notice what you're thinking and give it a quick label (planning, worrying, remembering, judging, etc.), then you can let it go and bring your focus back to your breath without judging yourself. You'll find you enjoy the practice of meditation more if you do this, and it brings your awareness to your higher self, the observer inside of you that is connected to the one universal energy.

3. High Expectations

Many people think that they have failed if they don't go into some kind of otherworldly feeling of transcendence. The truth is that you're not likely to experience that on most occasions when you meditate. What does happen though is that you are healing and balancing your chakras, which improves your physical, mental, and spiritual health, and you'll notice that it helps you stay grounded in the present moment even when you're not meditating. The practice of seeing and labeling your thoughts is key to this result. You'll start to notice that you can more easily let go of thoughts based in the past or the future, which helps you stay present. So, don't expect to be able to somehow rise above it all with each meditation, but each meditation will bring you closer to true connectedness and your higher self. Each meditation will also help balance your chakras.

4. Inconsistency

To get good at meditation, you need to be consistent about doing it. Your egoic mind will resist because it is what is threatened by your practice. As a result, it will throw up numerous barriers to a successful practice. You'll often find various parts of your body starting to itch, or you'll experience a need to sneeze, or you'll get a cramp, and all of these are mere distractions. It's your egoic mind trying to keep you from making that connection with your higher self. By meditating consistently, you'll begin to recognize those sensations as the distractions they are, and you'll start to understand how to overcome them. The key is awareness and staying grounded in the present moment. If you train yourself to notice them, you'll find they aren't enduring. Consistency is the key to developing this skill.

5. Judgmental You

Judgment is a useless activity. It's a habit that develops from other parts of your life, but when you bring it into your meditation practice, it's extremely counterproductive to successfully opening your chakras. A better habit is to use positive affirmations to replace any judgmental thoughts that arise. Notice those judgments and envision them rising and dissipating in the air the way smoke rising from a campfire does. Then, replace the thought with a positive affirmation like, "I'm getting better in meditative practice with each session," or, "I'm balancing and opening my chakras with each meditation practice." Soon, the judgmental thoughts will be a thing of the past.

6. Preconceived Notions

When you begin a meditation session with preconceived ideas about what you will achieve, you're not staying open to the experience, and you're not staying in the moment. As with high expectations, put aside any expectations and let the experience unfold organically. Be in harmony with what you're sensing, and you'll find your chakras will blossom.

Avoiding Mistakes

To help avoid making these mistakes and successfully open and harmonize your chakras, there are several things you can do before, during, and after your meditation practice. These will help set your practice up for success. Let's look at these helpful habits.

1. **Choose an appropriate environment:** For successful meditation, you need to be in a comfortable setting. That might mean a cozy room or a place out in nature where you can be alone and where it's silent outside of natural sounds. You'll also want to have on comfortable clothing, so you're not distracted by itchy material or something like tight pants. You also want to have a comfortable place to sit, perhaps a blanket or a cushion.
2. **Review your chakras from the bottom up:** You want to review your chakras to determine if they are blocked or have other problems. It might be obvious beforehand, but sometimes a problem could be caused by a problem in more than one chakra, and it will be necessary to discover each one by tuning into them one at a time. To review them, start with the root chakra and move upward, ending at the crown chakra. This means going from the most 'primitive' chakra

(concerned with basic survival) to the most highly developed chakra (concerned with consciousness).

3. **Re-energize each chakra:** Once you've reviewed your chakras, you'll begin the re-energizing process. Envision the chakras as lotus flowers, and as you breathe in, visualize light flowing into the chakra until it glows. As you breathe out, envision your stress flowing out of the chakra. Repeat this as often as necessary and then move on to the next chakra.
4. **Align the chakras:** To align the chakras, you want to get them to all rotate clockwise. If a chakra is spinning in the wrong direction or if it stops spinning, it can cause physical, mental, or
5. **Come out of your meditation slowly:** Once you have energized the last chakra, the crown chakra, continue to breathe deeply for several breaths, and slowly open your eyes to bring yourself out of your meditation. Don't rush it; let yourself be aware of your physical sensations and thoughts and emotions as you come out of the meditative state.
6. **Journal:** After finishing your meditation, it is helpful to journal about your physical sensations, your emotions, and your thoughts. It's also beneficial to journal daily to document your experiences as your chakras are balanced and open. This will help you know when they might be having problems again too.

Now that you know the basics of the process, it's helpful to go through a few guided meditations. It's important to realize that your experience with this type of meditation is different for each person and each sitting. If you're more of a visual person, it will be essential to use the colors associated with each chakra as a focal point. Other people who are more tactile might benefit from placing a hand at each chakra location. That can help them focus on the chakra while meditating.

It's also important to realize that meditation does not necessarily require that you close your eyes. Closing your eyes is typically used to help you soften your mind and focus. Still, some people might prefer lighting and candle and looking at that during meditation, only closing their eyes at the end of the practice. You might also like to use a visual cue of the chakra points to locate the points on your body. When you reach the crown, close your eyes. Maybe audio is more your style, and if that is the case, you can listen to a guided meditation or soothing music as you practice. With that, let's look at a couple of examples of guided chakra meditations.

Chakra Meditation #1

- Get comfortable: Find your spot and settle in. Make sure you won't be disturbed. Talk with your family about giving you this important time for self-care so that they know to leave you alone as you're practicing your meditation. Sit with your spine in an erect position and cross your legs in front of you. If this is uncomfortable for you, you can sit in a chair with your spine erect or on a meditation cushion. You want to sit in a comfortable position, where you won't be in danger of falling asleep, another problem to avoid to energize your chakras truly.

- Deep breaths: If you're not using a visual aid, close your eyes, and breathe in and out deeply so that your belly and chest expand and contract with each breath. Let your body relax. Physically scan and relax each part of your body, starting with your head and going down to your feet. Relax each part as you breathe deeply.

- Bring awareness to your chakras: Begin with the root chakra and create that mental image of energy flowing through it as it rotates clockwise. Envision each chakra in the color with which it is associated, and envision that energy circulating throughout your body, rising through the successive chakras to the crown chakra.

- Take your time with each chakra: Don't try to rush through envisioning the energetic wheels of health and wellness. Give yourself enough time to thoroughly visualize each of the seven main chakras rotating and sending energy flowing throughout your body.

- Envision the entire chakra system: Once you've envisioned each of the chakras individually, now you can visualize the whole system working together as the seamlessly flow of energy from your root chakra to your crown chakra, circulating throughout your body, leaving an effect on every part with which it comes into contact. Envision your entire body vibrating with life force energy.

- Express gratitude: Express gratitude for your body and the qi energy that infuses it. Let the feeling of appreciation flood your body and fill the chakras as it merges with your life force energy.

- Bring your meditation session to a close: Bring your focus back to your breath and focus once again on taking deep breaths. When you're ready, open your eyes. Before getting up from your sitting position, take note of the energetic feelings in your body.

- Journal about your experience: Write down your physical sensations, thoughts, and emotions as you went through this energizing experience.

Chakra Meditation #2

For this meditation, you may choose between sitting on the floor or lying flat.

- Get in your preferred position and bring your focus to your breath.

- Close your eyes as you pull your attention within to focus on your root chakra. This chakra represents your connection to the earth. Ask the universal energy to show you this association in whichever manner is best for you, perhaps a word, symbol, or color.

- After visualizing the association, bring your focus to the chakra and visualize it as a spinning wheel. Look deeply into the flow as it rotates. Breathe into the light of the chakra as well as space. Observe and trust that what is right for you will be shown to you. Allow your breath to expand the chakra's light, and brightness, the brighter, the better as this is a cleansing light. Visualize the chakra spinning in a clockwise direction and feel its warmth or coolness. Send every breath into that spinning wheel to expand and cleanse this powerful source of qi.

- Next, move your attention up to each successive chakra in the line. Again, take your time with each as you repeat the visualization listed in the step above. Some chakras will require more love on different days, so take your time. There is no rush. You are in the present moment, and all is well.

- When you reach the crown chakra, allow yourself to step into your mind's eye, and witness your entire body's living energy source. Scan your body to ensure that everything is open and aligned, and the energy is flowing freely. Breathe once again into every point, allowing your breath to move from the crown down the body, passing through each chakra to the base and back up again. Feel yourself in the flow of qi, and drink in the pleasure as your astral body is flowing with vitality.

- Trust yourself to know where you need to spend more time, and spend the time expanding each point. Remember that some will be more resistant than others. With each meditation session, you'll witness the differences in your body.

- If you have a specific area that you wish to focus on emotionally, spend time on that by concentrating your efforts on that chakra. For example, if you feel a need to expand your voice, you would choose to focus on the throat chakra, and as you do so, you can add a mantra: "I am releasing all that binds me. I center myself and allow myself to be in the flow of the universal oneness."

- When you have finished focusing on any specific areas you want to improve, bring your focus back to your breath. Once again, express gratitude for your life and the energy that flows through you. When you are ready, open your eyes.

Chakra Meditation #3

- Sit in a comfortable position with an erect spine, but do not make your spine rigid. Close your eyes and focus on your breath. Breathe deeply to expand your belly and chest.

- Bring your focus to each part of your body, beginning with your feet and working your way up. Have each part of the body relax as the stress melts away. Visualize the stress running off of your body as water running over and away from you.

● Focus again on your breath. Let it become steady and deep, but don't force it to be any particular way. Just breathe in fully in a non-forced manner. As your mind wanders, gently notice your thoughts, label them, and bless them as you let them go. Then, bring your mind back to your breath, focusing on each inhalation and exhalation. Visualize the oxygen filling your lungs and crossing over into the bloodstream. See it nourishing your muscles, organs, and cells, and watch as it removes toxins from your body, and these are expelled with each exhalation.

● Next, visualize the beating of your heart and the functioning of various parts of your body. Watch as everything works in perfect synchronicity as your breath sustains each area. Notice how the breath is the life-giving force for the entire body.

● Now, imagine the qi as part of what you are breathing in along with the air. Imagine this is a yellowish-orange colored stream that you pull into your body with every breath. Watch as it spreads throughout all areas of the body and infuses your aura. Imagine the aura growing stronger, brighter, and more energetically charged by this life force. Take your time with this visualization. Allow the aura to increase a little with each breath.

● Next, energize each chakra, beginning with the root chakra and working your way up. Visualize the clockwise swirling energy that grows stronger and brighter with each breath you take. At the same time, you're envisioning your life force breathing in with the air, visualizing another fountain of qi coming up from the earth, and adding to the swirling chakra energy.

- Move up to the sacral chakra and each successive chakra after that until you come to the crown chakra. Infuse each with the life force of qi. Spend all the time you need doing this, always working from the bottom up.

- Next, visualize all of the chakras being fed by the energy coming from the breath and the earth. Watch as your aura becomes brighter, clearer, and more energized. See the flow of energy passing through and around your body.

- Finally, bring your focus back to your breath and relax your body. When you are ready, open your eyes. Take a few moments to journal how you feel and the sensations you experienced with this process.

These three chakra meditations will cleanse and energize your chakras, thereby infusing your body with qi's life-giving energy. You'll experience numerous benefits with regular meditative practices. You'll see that you are actively exploring your entire body, witnessing the effects of your thoughts and feelings, and healing the imbalances that life throws your way. It's an incredibly personal practice that produces a profound sense of contentment, peace, and a sense of being energized. You'll find you're sleeping better and that you have a much better connection with your mind, body, and spirit. You also experience the interconnectedness of all things. Your chakras are a veritable tool kit for healing blockages of qi and restoring balance to your energy. That's why it is vital to nurture a harmonious chakra system.

Remember that the purpose of working with your chakras is to experience the wholeness within yourself. As you regularly practice these meditations, you'll bring all aspects of your consciousness—spiritual, emotional, mental, and physical—into harmonious balance. You'll be able to witness the benefits of your entire system working together as you acknowledge and integrate all levels of your being. Those swirling wheels of energy contain not only bundles of physical structures like nerves and organs, but they also hold your psychological, emotional, and spiritual states of being. Because all of these elements are always moving, you must keep the chakras open, aligned, and fluid. Blockages cause the energy to back up and stagnate, and that is when illness can occur. Everything is connected, and when you can reach inside yourself to see the flow of your life force, you'll realize the importance of maintaining the balance and harmony of every aspect of the system. When you're in harmony, you're better able to experience the life flow of the universe as it cycles through you and every other thing, you'll experience unity with all things, and as a result, your compassion, love, and abundance will blossom.

Seven Powerful Crystals Every Empath Should Have

Are you feeling overwhelmed with other people's emotions?

Would you like to protect and heal your energy?

Being an empath means absorbing both the positive and negative energies

This can be both a blessing and a curse

The good news is that crystals with their unique characteristics and vibration can actually help

To balance your emotions, protect your energy and keep you grounded with these 7 powerful crystals, visit: https://bit.ly/2Y8cIkp

Resources

Ageless Arts. (2018, February 28). Sa Ta Na Ma Meditation, a powerful tool for preventing or stopping Alzheimer's disease. Retrieved February 11, 2020, from https://agelessartsyoga.com/instructor-group-yoga/sa-ta-na-ma-meditation/

Critcher, C. R., & Dunning, D. (2014). Self-Affirmations Provide a Broader Perspective on Self-Threat. *Personality and Social Psychology Bulletin, 41*(1), 3–18. https://doi.org/10.1177/0146167214554956

Eisler, M. (2017, January 23). How to Stay Emotionally Balanced If You're an Empath. Retrieved February 4, 2020, from https://chopra.com/articles/how-to-stay-emotionally-balanced-if-you%E2%80%99re-an-empath

Ewens, H. (2018, November 8). Super Empaths Are Real, Says Study. Retrieved February 11, 2020, from https://www.vice.com/en_us/article/xwj84k/super-empaths-are-real-says-study

Familydoctor.org editorial staff. (2019, July 22). Mind/Body Connection: How Emotions Affect Health. Retrieved February 3, 2020, from https://familydoctor.org/mindbody-connection-how-your-emotions-affect-your-health/

Grace, S. (2019, January 8). How To Eat To Thrive as an Empath. Retrieved February 11, 2020, from https://www.sarahkgrace.com/blog/how-to-eat-to-thrive-as-an-empath

Greenberg, E. (2018, July 8). How to Avoid Toxic Relationships Try these five tips when you are choosing friends and mates. Retrieved February 11, 2020, from https://www.psychologytoday.com/us/blog/understanding-narcissism/201807/how-avoid-toxic-relationships

Gulla, A. (2017, November 14). 15 Things To Remember If You Love An Empath. Retrieved February 11, 2020, from https://www.lifehack.org/articles/communication/15-tips-help-you-love-empath.html

Holland, K. (2019, August 15). How to Recognize and Respond to Energy Vampires at Home, Work, and More. Retrieved February 11, 2020, from https://www.healthline.com/health/mental-health/energy-vampires#codependent

Howe, M. (2018, December 6). Energy & Empaths - National Wellness Institute. Retrieved February 11, 2020, from https://www.nationalwellness.org/blogpost/1644820/314421/Energy—Empaths

Hutchison, L. H. (2016, January 25). Exercise for Empaths: Let's Get Physical! Retrieved February 11, 2020, from https://connectingempathichelpersandartiststospirit.wordpress.com/2016/01/05/exercise-for-empaths-lets-get-physical/

Kathrine, D. (2019, August 3). Navigating Psychic Attack: A Guide for The Empath. Retrieved February 11, 2020, from https://theknowing1.wordpress.com/2013/11/13/navigating-psychic-attack/

Luna, A. (2020, January 18). How Being an Empath is Connected to Spiritually Awakening ⋆. Retrieved February 11, 2020, from https://lonerwolf.com/being-an-empath-awakening/

Magine, S. (2018, September 18). What is an Empath? Empathy, Energy and the Spectrum of Sensitivity. Retrieved February 11, 2020, from https://mechanicsofbeing.com/empath-energy-coping-spectrum-of-sensitivity/

Marciniak, R., Sheardova, K., Čermáková, P., Hudeček, D., Šumec, R., & Hort, J. (2014). Effect of Meditation on Cognitive Functions in Context of Aging and Neurodegenerative Diseases. *Frontiers in Behavioral Neuroscience*, 8. https://doi.org/10.3389/fnbeh.2014.00017

Mystical Raven. (2019, February 6). Being An Empath Is Connected To A Powerful Spiritual Awakening. Retrieved February 11, 2020, from https://mysticalraven.com/spirituality/14548/being-an-empath-is-connected-to-a-powerful-spiritual-awakening

Nicely Done Magick. (n.d.). Empowered Empaths. Retrieved February 11, 2020, from https://www.nicelydonemagick.com/empowered-empaths.html

Orloff, J. (2014, December 2). 6 Relationship Tips for Empaths. Retrieved February 11, 2020, from https://www.elephantjournal.com/2014/12/6-relationship-tips-for-empaths/

Orloff, J. (2016, February 19). 10 Traits Empathic People Share And how to look out for yourself if you are one. Retrieved February 11, 2020, from https://www.psychologytoday.com/us/blog/emotional-freedom/201602/10-traits-empathic-people-share

Orloff, J. (2018, July 3). Are You an Introverted or Extroverted Empath? Retrieved February 11, 2020, from https://drjudithorloff.com/ask-dr-orloff/are-all-empaths-introverts/

Orloff, J. (2019, September 23). Are You an Empath? Take this 20 Question Empath Test. Retrieved February 11, 2020, from https://drjudithorloff.com/quizzes/empath-self-assessment-test/

Planetary Cymatic Resonance. (n.d.). Planetary Cymatic Resonance - BRAINWAVE STIMULATION & THERAPEUTIC SOUND Meditation. Retrieved February 4, 2020, from http://www.gravityterminal.com/event/planetary-cymatic-resonance-brainwave-stimulation-therapeutic-sound

Pursey, K. (2018, November 23). 6 Types of Empaths: Which One Are You and How to Make the Most of Your Gift? Retrieved February 11, 2020, from https://www.learning-mind.com/types-of-empaths/

Raghu, M. (2018). A Study to Explore the Effects of Sound Vibrations on Consciousness. *International Journal of Social Work and Human Services Practice*, *6*(3), 75–88. Retrieved from http://www.hrpub.org/download/20180730/IJRH2-19290514.pdf

Sacred Acoustics. (n.d.). Technology - Sacred Acoustics. Retrieved February 4, 2020, from https://www.sacredacoustics.com/pages/technology-app

Sage Goddess. (2019, March 28). What is Smudging and How do I Smudge? Retrieved February 11, 2020, from https://www.sagegoddess.com/how-do-i-smudge/

Soldner, J. (2017, June 18). Empaths and the Law of Attraction. Retrieved February 11, 2020, from http://www.jennifersoldner.com/2016/09/empaths-and-the-law-of-attraction.html

Stewart, E. (2016a, June 12). Empaths and Manifesting Part 1. Retrieved February 11, 2020, from https://psychicspiritart.com/2016/06/05/empaths-and-manifesting-part-1/

Stewart, E. (2016b, June 12). Empaths and Manifesting Part 2. Retrieved February 11, 2020, from https://psychicspiritart.com/2016/06/08/empaths-and-manifesting-part-2/

Tartakovsky, M. M. S. (2018, October 8). 10 Way to Build and Preserve Better Boundaries. Retrieved February 11, 2020, from https://psychcentral.com/lib/10-way-to-build-and-preserve-better-boundaries/

Team Empathy. (2018, February 13). 50 Ways To Ground Yourself As An Empath. Retrieved February 11, 2020, from https://enlightenedempathy.wordpress.com/2018/02/12/50-ways-to-ground-yourself-as-an-empath/

Tedder, L. (2018, June 8). What Energetic Connections Feel Like to an Empath. Retrieved February 11, 2020, from https://www.thespiritualeclectic.com/2014/05/06/what-energetic-connections-feel-like-to-an-empath/

The International Center for Reiki Training. (2019, September 11). What is Reiki? Retrieved February 11, 2020, from https://www.reiki.org/faqs/what-reiki

Unknown, I. (2019, July 8). Binaural Beats. Retrieved February 4, 2020, from https://www.empathguide.com/binaural-beats/

Wiest, B. (2018, October 17). 16 Signs You're Having What's Known As A Kundalini Awakening. Retrieved February 11, 2020, from https://thoughtcatalog.com/brianna-wiest/2018/08/16-signs-youre-having-whats-known-as-a-kundalini-awakening/

Don't miss out!

Visit the website below and you can sign up to receive emails whenever Alison L. Alverson publishes a new book. There's no charge and no obligation.

https://books2read.com/r/B-A-RQLJ-TVMGB

BOOKS2READ

Connecting independent readers to independent writers.

Did you love *Empath Workbook: Discover 50 Successful Tips To Boost your Emotional, Physical And Spiritual Energy*? Then you should read *Chakra Healing For Beginners: The Complete Guide to Awaken and Balance Chakras for Self-Healing and Positive Energy* by Alison L. Alverson!

In a universe made of energy...

...how you control your own is essential.

Are you ready to expand your health and happiness?

To awaken, one must understand the power of the chakras. To heal one's mind, body, and spirit, one must align them. The wonders of a quiet mind allow anyone to achieve a level of joy and abundance they never knew existed.

This journey will change your life.

You'll learn:

♦ Ancient Medicine and the Use of Chakras

- Secret and Powerful Healing Techniques
- Six Mistakes Most Beginners Make in Meditation and How to Avoid Them
- How Guided Meditation Can Transform and Awaken You Spiritually
- The Mysteries and Benefits of Hindu and Buddhist Tantras
- plus, much more

Alison L. Alverson is an accomplished self-published author. She is an empath, who has spent nearly one decade, since awakening, mastering the practices. Each day will be one you can cherish once you've brought your life into alignment.

It's time to unleash the power of your chakras.

You'll love these lessons because improving your mental and physical well-being is the best thing you can do for yourself.

Get started now!

Read more at www.alisonalverson.com.

Also by Alison L. Alverson

Chakra Series Book 1
Chakra Healing For Beginners: The Complete Guide to Awaken and Balance Chakras for Self-Healing and Positive Energy

Chakra Series Book 2
Chakra Healing For Beginners: Discover 35 Self-Healing Techniques to Awaken and Balance Chakras for Health and Positive Energy

Empath Series Book 1
Empath: An Extensive Guide for Developing Your Gift of Intuition to Thrive in Life

Empath Series Book 2
Empath Workbook: Discover 50 Successful Tips To Boost your Emotional, Physical And Spiritual Energy

Standalone

Emotional Intelligence : 21 Effective Tips To Boost Your EQ (A Practical Guide To Mastering Emotions, Improving Social Skills & Fulfilling Relationships For A Happy And Successful Life)

Watch for more at www.alisonalverson.com.

About the Author

Alison L. Alverson is an American and accomplished self-published author. She is an empath, who has spent nearly one decade, since awakening, mastering her empathic nature. She studied various psychological techniques and attended spiritual healing workshops from a variety of traditions.

She has a burning passion and an open spirit to help empaths, who are the healers, the nurturers, and the highly sensitive persons, manage their empathy without getting drained and teach them strategies to thrive as an empath by sharing with them her experiences and practical tips that helped her. She wants to grow continuously, and she wants to encourage empaths to do the same through taking consistent actions.

Alison loves to travel and finds her passion in writing books. She is a social person and loves sitting with people and listening to them. In her free time, she likes taking photos, especially outdoors, and listening to the sound of nature. Alison loves to hear from her dear readers.

Feel free to email her at alisonalverson12@gmail.com

Read more at www.alisonalverson.com.

CPSIA information can be obtained
at www.ICGtesting.com
Printed in the USA
LVHW080000090222
710650LV00013B/675